The whaleS Companion

The whaleS Companion

The whale in legend, art and literature

EDITED BY

ARIANA KLEPAC

Ww Ww

Contents

W. was a whale,
Who lived in the sea,
And swam all about
As far as could be.

12345

INTRODUCTION

Everything about a whale is big and, correspondingly, human responses to the whale, in both pictures and words, have always been equally dramatic – whether it be curiosity about the exact nature of these fishlike mammals, delight at their unusual shape and size, greed for what riches their slaughter might bring, fear of their potential power, or sadness at the thought of their decline and death. When these fellow mammals sing their songs, we crave their lyrics as if their messages might unlock secrets of a parallel world under the sea, and when they breach and dive we are entranced by their majestic beauty and size. We have simultaneously worshipped and coveted one of the greatest miracles on earth.

THE TRUE FORM OF THE WHALE Whales are the largest animals ever to have graced our planet – larger even than any dinosaur – with the blue whale the supreme species, at 30 metres (98 feet) in length and a weight of 200 tonnes (tons) These remarkable animals are found in all seas and oceans, from the equator to the poles. Their life expectancy is around 30 to 90 years; however, in 2007 the fragment of a nineteenth-century whaler's bow lance was found inside a bowhead whale, which suggests that the whale may have been as old as 130 years.

Although referred to as a 'great fish' for centuries, whales are mammals who, like us, breathe the air, suckle their young on milk, and are warm-blooded. However, these mammals, who are descended from land-dwellers, have been entirely aquatic for

50 million years, and have developed flippers and tail flukes to propel them through life in the water, to depths of up to 3000 metres (9843 feet). Interestingly, some species still have rudimentary hind limbs, with recognisable feet and toes.

It seems amazing that these air-breathers could survive in the water. But survive they do, with hearts that can be the size of a small car, pumping up to 1500 litres (2640 pints) of blood around their bodies. The whale is without doubt an incredible feat of engineering.

In order to breathe, whales must rise to the surface in order to take a gulp of air, which can last them for as long as two hours. However, before they breathe in, they must empty their lungs of air with a huge outburst of breath, known as the 'blow'. As the breath is warmer than the surrounding air, it condenses to look like a spout of water.

Whales are divided into two groups, depending on how they feed, namely baleen or toothed whales. The massive baleen whales – such as blue, fin, humpback and right whales – suck in seawater and, through sieve-like structures called baleen plates, they filter out food in the form of krill and other tiny crustaceans. The smaller, toothed whales – such as belugas, narwhals and pilot, sperm and killer whales – have teeth and feed on larger prey like fish and squid.

IF WHALES COULD TALK As well as their spectacular size, it is the haunting song of the whale that has often captured the human imagination. In addition to many noises, such as clicking, wheezing, whistling and groaning, whales, such as the humpback, create songs. These 'songs' may be mating calls, but might also be signals to other whales not to trespass on their territory, or to tell their fellow pod-members that it is time to migrate. Not only do whale sounds and songs have beauty, they also have power – the sounds of the fin whale can travel more than 1800 kilometres (1120 miles).

However, with the whale's immense dimensions and power, comes fragility. If a whale is stranded on land it could mean a death sentence, as the mammal's huge bodyweight could crush its lungs and suffocate it. Unable to shift their huge bulk back into the life-giving water, whales often dehydrate and die.

These strandings, of sometimes just one whale, sometimes a whole pod of hundreds, are a phenomenon that has many possible explanations. Whales use the earth's magnetic field to guide them. These fields tend to fluctuate, but solar activity can create irregular fluctuations that confuse the whales and cause strandings. On the other hand, disease or parasitic infection in the brain may be the reason behind whales losing their sense of direction.

A SURE PRIZE The plight of the whale is inextricably linked to that of humans, who have hunted the mammals as a source of food and resources for thousands of years. There is an image of a whale tethered to a boatload of men — possibly hunters — on a sandstone wall in Korea, dating back to around 6000 BC; the Norwegians practised whaling from about 4000 BC; and the remains of ancient villages made from whalebone have been found in Greenland.

Early whaling was generally in the form of subsistence hunting. And it was the people of the north coast of North America who were the masters of this art (in fact, some of their methods were used right up to the beginning of the twentieth century in the commercial whaling industry). As the polar landscape did not offer much in the way of food, the tribes were forced to look to the sea for sustenance. There is evidence that whaling began in the Bering and Chukchi seas about 2000 years ago. A beached whale would have meant easy food for a whole tribe. However, the Thule people of northern Alaska, around AD 800, took to the water in pursuit of the mammal. In addition to food, the whales provided oil for lamps and bones for weapons and building materials.

But the forerunners of commercial whaling were undoubtedly the Basques who, by the fourteenth century, were unrivalled in their whale-hunting techniques. They specialised in hunting the right whale and, as early as the fifteenth century, numbers of this whale began dropping significantly. The archives of Lekeitio in Spain, in the Bay of Biscay, recorded forty-eight kills between 1517 and 1661. Therefore it wasn't overhunting causing the drop in whale numbers; in fact it was the advent of a mini ice-age, which lasted for the remainder of the seventeenth century.

In 1610, the English had begun whaling around the island of Spitsbergen in the Arctic Ocean, but the Dutch were soon in fierce competition. Whaling in this area was thriving by the 1630s and 1640s, and Smeerenburg on Amsterdam Island was better known as 'Blubbertown'. During the 'Little Ice-Age', the whaling moved into the open sea ice, and then further into the Davis Strait, where whaling was dominated by the Dutch and Germans until the 1780s.

Fishing had begun in the British North American colonies in the 1690s, but in 1712 the first sperm whale was caught by a Nantucket vessel from Massachusetts, and the areas of Cape Cod, Rhode Island and Long Island became the new centre of the whaling world. Nowhere can we get a more accurate and colourful account of this period, than in Herman Melville's novel *Moby Dick* (1851).

During the eighteenth and nineteenth centuries, the whaling industry continued to thrive and improvements were made to whaling vessels. The invention of the harpoon cannon in 1863 made it possible to catch the enormous rorqual whales, such as the blue whale, who had previously just sunk when harpooned.

TOMBSTONE FOR A WHALE Up until the beginning of the twentieth century, the battle between hunted and hunter was fairly evenly pitched. However, with the introduction of ever more efficient hunting machinery, the number of whales killed per season increased. In 1885 thirty whaling vessels killed 1287 whales. In the period between World War I and World War II, when whales were in demand for glycerin for explosives, 50,000 whales were decimated. With the invention of the 'factory ship' came the ability to hunt even more whales. By 1962, an astounding 73,502 whales were killed in a single season — and this was sadly sixteen years after the International Whaling Commission (IWC) was established to 'save the whale'.

The League of Nations had first moved to regulate whaling in 1931, but it was not until 1946 that the IWC was officially established to conserve numbers. In 1972 the United Nations proposed a moratorium on whaling, but the motion was quashed. Finally, in 1979 the use of factory ships was banned for all whales except minke. During the whaling seasons of 1986–90, the world agreed to a complete moratorium on all commercial whaling, to allow time to take stock of the situation. This moratorium has never been revoked, but at the time this book was published, some Japanese and Norwegian whaling still continues, to the great anger and shame of many of us who share this planet.

Created as a celebration of the whale, this book is a collection of writings from ancient and modern scientific sources, literature, philosophy, mythology, folklore, religious texts and whalers' journals. From the vengeful cries of Herman Melville's Captain Ahab, pursuing the white whale Moby Dick to the ends of the earth and his own simultaneous destruction, to Tim Winton's passionate plea to end whale hunting, the words of these great writers and thinkers resonate deeply within us and demonstrate the immense power of this magnificent mammal, which will always hold a special place in the human imagination and psyche.

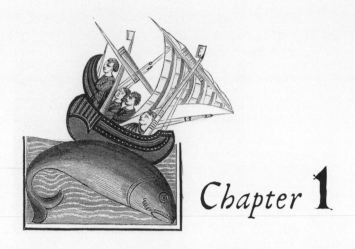

Chapter **1**

WHAT *like* IS A WHALE?

Defining the whale

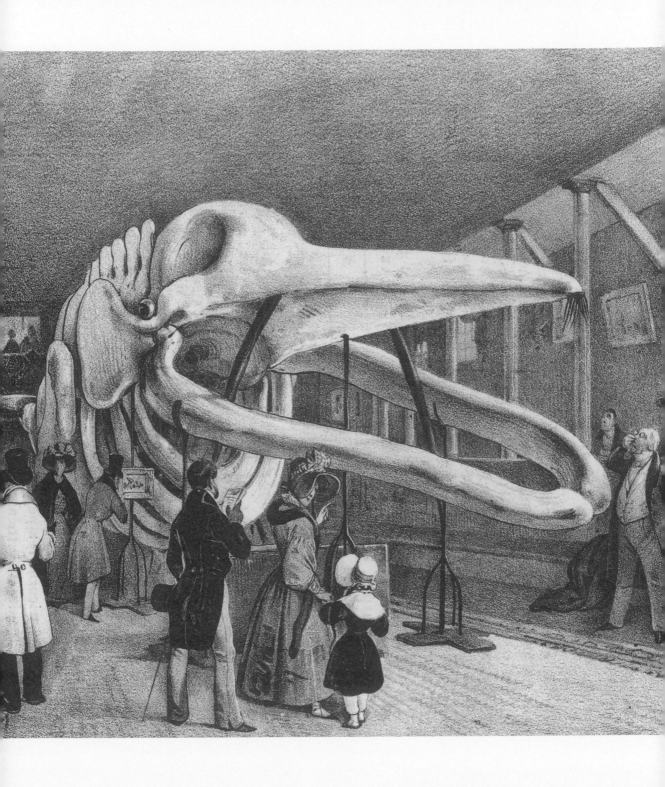

Variously known as a sea monster, a spirit of the sea, an earthly incarnation of a god, or an idea 'too absurd to be true', the whale has been an object of wonder for humans for thousands of years. By the time of Greek philosopher Aristotle (384–322 BC), it was already known that the whale was not in fact a fish, but rather a marine mammal and fellow air-breather. Even so, 400 years after Aristotle's observations, Plutarch refers to a whale as a 'monster', and 1800 years later Dutch beachcomber Adriaen Coenen, in his *Whale Book*, still thought of the creature as an enormous fish. Possibly the centuries-long confusion about the precise nature of a whale may have been because the whale was difficult to observe in its entirety; sightings mainly being just of the parts, rather than the whole — the blowhole spouting air, or the enormous flukes disappearing under the water. And for those most interested in seeing a whale, namely whalers and hunters, time was spent not on watching and wondering, but rather on readying the harpoon. It wasn't until the twentieth century that humans sought out whales in a spirit of friendship and curiosity, observing these marvellous animals in their natural habitat.

Chief among these motives was the overwhelming idea of the great whale himself. Such a portentous and mysterious monster roused all my curiosity. Then the wild and distant seas where he rolled his island bulk; the undeliverable, nameless perils of the whale; these, with all the attending marvels of a thousand Patagonian sights and sounds, helped to sway me to my wish.

Herman Melville, *Moby Dick*, 1851

So, fire with water to compare,
The ocean serves on high,

Up-spouted by a whale in air,
To express unwieldy joy.

William Cowper, 'On the Queen's Visit to London', 1789

Of the Monstrous
Pictures of Whales

I shall ere long paint to you as well as one can without canvas, something like the true form of the whale as he actually appears to the eye of the whaleman when in his own absolute body the whale is moored alongside the whale-ship so that he can be fairly stepped upon there. It may be worth while, therefore, previously to advert to those curious imaginary portraits of him which even down to the present day confidently challenge the faith of the landsman. It is time to set the world right in this matter, by proving such pictures of the whale all wrong.

It may be that the primal source of all those pictorial delusions will be found among the oldest Hindoo, Egyptian, and Grecian sculptures. For ever since those inventive but unscrupulous times when on the marble panellings of temples, the pedestals of statues, and on shields, medallions, cups, and coins, the dolphin was drawn in scales of chain-armor like Saladin's, and a helmeted head like St. George's; ever since then has something of the same sort of license prevailed, not only in most popular pictures of the whale, but in many scientific presentations of him.

Now, by all odds, the most ancient extant portrait anyways purporting to be the whale's, is to be found in the famous cavern-pagoda of Elephanta, in India. The Brahmins maintain that in the almost endless sculptures of that immemorial pagoda, all the trades and pursuits, every conceivable avocation of man, were prefigured ages before any of them actually came into being. No wonder then, that in some sort our noble profession of whaling should have been there shadowed forth.

Herman Melville, *Moby Dick*, 1851

The first time I saw a whale

R. M. Ballantyne,
Fighting the Whales, 1915

I shall never forget the surprise I got the first time I saw a whale.

It was in the forenoon of a most splendid day, about a week after we arrived at that part of the ocean where we might expect to find fish. A light nor'-east breeze was blowing, but it scarcely ruffled the sea, as we crept slowly through the water with every stitch of canvas set.

As we had been looking out for fish for some time past, everything was in readiness for them. The boats were hanging over the side ready to lower, tubs for coiling away the ropes, harpoons, lances, &c., all were ready to throw in, and start away at a moment's notice. The man in the 'crow's-nest', as they call the cask fixed up at the masthead, was looking anxiously out for whales, and the crew were idling about the deck. Tom Lokins was seated on the windlass smoking his pipe, and I was sitting beside him on an empty cask, sharpening a blubber-knife.

'Tom,' said I, 'what like is a whale?'.

'Why, it's like nothin' but itself,' replied Tom, looking puzzled.

'Why, wot a queer feller you are to ax questions.'

'I'm sure you've seen plenty of them. You might be able to tell what a whale is like.'

'Wot it's like! Well, it's like a tremendous big bolster with a head and a tail to it.'

'And how big is it?'.

'They're of all sizes, lad. I've seen one that was exactly equal to three hundred fat bulls, and its rate of goin' would take it round the whole world in twenty-three days.'

'I don't believe you,' said I, laughing.

'Don't you?' cried Tom; 'it's a fact notwithstandin', for the captain himself said so, and that's how I came to know it'.

Just as Tom finished speaking, the man in the crow's-nest roared at the top of his voice, 'There she blows!'

That was the signal that a whale was in sight, and as it was the first time we had heard it that season, every man in the ship was thrown into a state of tremendous excitement.

'There she blows!' roared the man again.

'Where away?' shouted the captain.

'About two miles right ahead.'

In another moment the utmost excitement prevailed on board. Suddenly, while I was looking over the side, straining my eyes to catch a sight of the whale, which could not yet be seen by the men on deck, I saw a brown object appear in the sea, not twenty yards from the side of the ship; before I had time to ask what it was, a whale's head rose to the surface, and shot up out of the water. The part of the fish that was visible above water could not have been less than thirty feet in length. It just looked as if our longboat had jumped out of the sea, and he was so near that I could see his great mouth quite plainly. I could have tossed a biscuit on his back easily. Sending two thick spouts of frothy water out of his blow-holes forty feet into the air with tremendous noise, he fell flat upon the sea with a clap like thunder, tossed his flukes or tail high into the air, and disappeared.

I was so amazed at this sight that I could not speak. I could only stare at the place where the huge monster had gone down.

Etymology

(Supplied by a Late Consumptive Usher to a Grammar School)

The pale Usher — threadbare in coat, heart, body, and brain; I see him now. He was ever dusting his old lexicons and grammars, with a queer handkerchief, mockingly embellished with all the gay flags of all the known nations of the world. He loved to dust his old grammars; it somehow mildly reminded him of his mortality.

'While you take in hand to school others, and to teach them by what name a whale-fish is to be called in our tongue leaving out, through ignorance, the letter H, which almost alone maketh the signification of the word, you deliver that which is not true.'
— HACKLUYT

'WHALE. ... Sw. and Dan. HVAL. This animal is named from roundness or rolling; for in Dan. HVALT is arched or vaulted.'
— WEBSTER'S DICTIONARY

'WHALE. ... It is more immediately from the Dut. and Ger. WALLEN; A.S. WALW-IAN, to roll, to wallow.'
— RICHARDSON'S DICTIONARY

KETOS, Greek.

CETUS, Latin.

WHOEL, Anglo-Saxon.

HVALT, Danish.

WAL, Dutch.

HWAL, Swedish.

WHALE, Icelandic.

WHALE, English.

BALEINE, French.

BALLENA, Spanish.

PEKEE-NUEE-NUEE, Fegee.

PEKEE-NUEE-NUEE, Erromangoan.

Herman Melville,
Preface to *Moby Dick*, 1851

ARISTOTLE

describes the whale

AGAIN, SOME ANIMALS ARE VIVIPAROUS, OTHERS OVIPAROUS, OTHERS VERMIPAROUS OR 'GRUB-BEARING'. SOME ARE VIVIPAROUS, SUCH AS MAN, THE HORSE, THE SEAL, AND ALL OTHER ANIMALS THAT ARE HAIR-COATED, AND, OF MARINE ANIMALS, THE CETACEANS, AS THE DOLPHIN, AND THE SO-CALLED SELACHIA. (OF THESE LATTER ANIMALS, SOME HAVE A TUBULAR AIR-PASSAGE AND NO GILLS, AS THE DOLPHIN AND THE WHALE: THE DOLPHIN WITH THE AIR-PASSAGE GOING THROUGH ITS BACK, THE WHALE WITH THE AIR-PASSAGE IN ITS FOREHEAD; OTHERS HAVE UNCOVERED GILLS, AS THE SELACHIA, THE SHARKS AND RAYS.)

☙

THE DOLPHIN AND THE WHALE, AND ALL SUCH AS ARE FURNISHED WITH A BLOW-HOLE, SLEEP WITH THE BLOW-HOLE OVER THE SURFACE OF THE WATER, AND BREATHE THROUGH THE BLOW-HOLE WHILE THEY KEEP UP A QUIET FLAPPING OF THEIR FINS

Aristotle, *Historia Animalium (The History of Animals)*, c.343 BC

THE CHAOS OF THIS MONSTER'S MOUTH

And what thing soever besides cometh within the chaos of this monster's mouth, be it beast, boat, or stone, down it goes all incontinently that foul great swallow of his, and perisheth in the bottomless gulf of his paunch.

Plutarch, *Morals*, AD 100

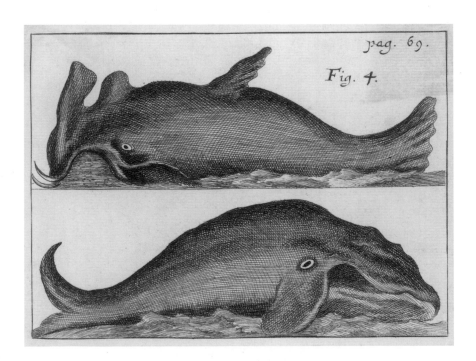

In their way they saw many whales sporting in the ocean, and in wantonness fuzzing up the water through their pipes and vents, which nature has placed on their shoulders.

Sir Thomas Herbert, *Voyages into Asia and Africa*, 1696

A most
monstrous
size.

Scarcely had we proceeded two days
on the sea, when about sunrise a great
many Whales and other monsters of
the sea, appeared. Among the former,
one was of a most monstrous size …
This came towards us, open-mouthed,
raising the waves on all sides, and
beating the sea before him into a foam.

Lucian of Samosata, *The True History*, AD 120–180

Fastitocalon

❧

NOW WILL I SPUR AGAIN MY WIT, AND USE

POETIC SKILL TO WEAVE WORDS INTO SONG,

TELLING OF ONE AMONG THE RACE OF FISH,

THE GREAT ASP-TURTLE. MEN WHO SAIL THE SEA

OFTEN UNWILLINGLY ENCOUNTER HIM,

DREAD PREYER ON MANKIND. HIS NAME WE KNOW,

THE OCEAN-SWIMMER, FASTITOCALON.

DUN, LIKE ROUGH STONE IN COLOR, AS HE FLOATS

HE SEEMS A HEAVING BANK OF REEDY GRASS

ALONG THE SHORE, WITH ROLLING DUNES BEHIND,

SO THAT SEA-WANDERERS DEEM THEIR GAZE HAS FOUND

AN ISLAND. BOLDLY THEN THEIR HIGH-PROWED SHIPS

THEY MOOR WITH CABLES TO THAT SHORE, A LAND

THAT IS NO LAND. STILL FLOATING ON THE WAVES,

THEIR OCEAN-COURSERS CURVET AT THE MARGE.

❧

The Physiologus, 2nd century

from

ADRIAEN COENEN'S

The Whale Book . . .

1585

Whale (walvis)

True-to-life portrait and dimensions of the fish caught on 2 July 1577. In the year of Our Lord 1577, on the day of 2 July, a living fish was caught between Haeften and Saaftinge in the river Schelde near Antwerp close to the dyke. It could not float there because the water was too shallow. It was finished off with picks, hooks and other instruments. It roared in a terrible fashion and made an enormous hullabaloo before it died, so that the water was tremendously stirred up, churned up and troubled from bottom to top. Afterwards it was dragged with ropes and small boats to Haeften.

Its skin had no scales and was like leather, as grey as lead. He was 58 feet long, 16 feet 3 thumbs high, and 12 feet broad. The distance from the tip of his mouth to the farthest point of his eyes was 15 feet, and 4 feet 3 thumbs from the eyes to the fin. The fins were 5 feet 2 thumbs long. He had 50 teeth in the lower jaw and there were 50 holes in the upper jaw into which the teeth fitted. His jaw was 7 thumbs wide at the tip, but 1 foot 6 thumbs at the back, with a length of 8 feet. The tongue lay in the throat like a liver and was the size of a barrel of beer. The tail was 14 feet 3 thumbs wide. And his penis was 8 feet long and tapering. Above his nose he had an opening or split, from which he spouted excess water. The boatmen who killed him called him a whale and said that there were two other dead near Bieselinge.

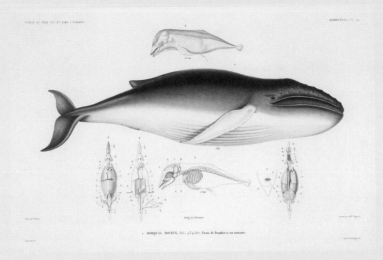

About a wondrous fish
that was found in North England in 1532

It was 90 feet long. In the harvest month of the year 1532, a very large and very rare monster was washed up on the shore of Tynemouth. It was partly torn, but there was still enough left to fill a hundred carts. According to the source on which this information is based, there was an intolerable stench on the 26th day of the harvest month, when the creature was still there. The beast had 30 ribs in its side, with a length of 21 feet, three stomachs the size of very deep cellars, thirty throats, of which 5 were very big, and 2 fins, each 15 feet long. Reports on its tongue vary, but most say it was 7 ells long. The teeth were like the horns of an animal and its eyes were small in proportion to the body. They said that its sheath was wondrously big, a male. When they were cutting the beast open someone almost drowned because he fell into its belly; he would have come to a bad end if he hadn't been able to grab a rib with his hand and hold on to that. After I had written this, I saw an illustration of this fish, and it looked exactly like the three fish that were beached near Westerheij in 1577.

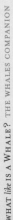

Sperm whale (potvis)

A potswal, called a potshooft by our fishers.

    This one of the three fish that were stranded near the village of Westerheij on 23 November 1577. They were remarkably big fish, all three male, and the same in appearance. They were lying about a broadside from one another on the beach when I saw them there. The largest was 55 feet, the second 49 feet, the third 48 feet.

    All three fish were black, the whole body as fat as a porpoise, but somewhat less fatty or oily in proportion to their size, and with rather more meat. They had short teeth in the lower jaws, which protruded like the horns of a young cow, and there were holes in the upper jaws into which the teeth fitted. They had small eyes considering their size, smaller than the eyes of a cow. All three had sheaths near the belly that were tapered like a bull's pizzle, and a very blunt head. Together these three fish raised 578 guilders, of which 12 guilders were given to the poor.

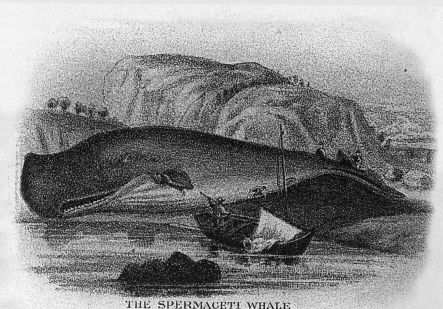

THE SPERMACETI WHALE

Baleen whale (balena)

This is a big whale that is called belua or balena as described below. Our fishers here give all rare big fish the following names in Dutch: a. walvissen, b. wilde belijen, c. hillen, d. westerlingen, e. potshoofden. The hillen have pointed heads, the potshoofden (sperm whales) have blunt heads, and the whales (walvissen) have pipes above the head from which they spout water.

The baleen whale is a very large beast in the sea and spouts a lot of water as if it were a cloud, which sometimes causes ships considerable trouble. The baleen whale is not seen until the winter comes. In the summer it is rarely seen; they lie hidden in their sweet meadows and that is where they give birth. And when they give birth they are in such pain that they come to the surface for help. They give birth just like the other large animals of the earth and sleep too. If a storm is brewing they shelter their young in their jaws and blow them out again once the storm is over. They reach adult length in two years.

The baleen whale is an extremely large fish that stirs up the sea with big waves and billows that come from the sea bed. They are a great danger to ships, as happened with the ships of Alexander the Great. There are many of this kind of fish in the Eastern Sea.

Balata is a beast of the sea and behaves contrary to nature compared with other animals, because when she feels the young in her belly she pulls them out. If they are fully grown she leaves them outside, but if they are still too small she puts them back in the belly to grow fully.

EN L AN 2000

Porphyrio THE WHALE

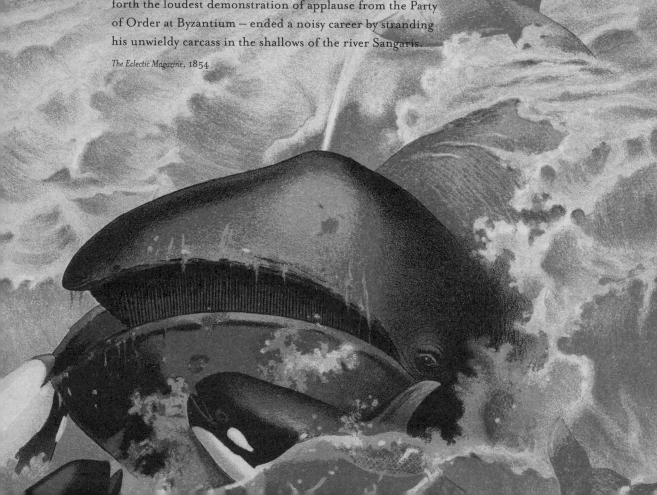

There is a lively anecdote told by that pleasing twaddler,
Procopius, which, though related of the age of Justinian,
embodies, with prophetic inspiration, an event we are all
anxiously awaiting. His Imperial Majesty had prepared
a palace and gardens not far from the Bosphorus, and
specially destined for the summer residence of the chaste
Theodora. But the nymphs of the delightful groves — so it
is complained by the historial — were often alarmed by the
misconduct of one Porphyrio, a whale ten cubits broad
and thirty long. This mammal, after passing a quarter of a
century in pompous manoeuvres — which doubtless called
forth the loudest demonstration of applause from the Party
of Order at Byzantium — ended a noisy career by stranding
his unwieldy carcass in the shallows of the river Sangaris.

The Eclectic Magazine, 1854

The whale and its guide

'Tis said that the whale never moves that she has not always before her a little fish like the sea-gudgeon, for this reason called the guide-fish, whom the whale follows, suffering himself to be led and turned with as great facility as the rudder guides the ship: in recompense of which service also, whereas all the other things, whether beast or vessel, that enter into the dreadful gulf of this monster's mouth, are immediately lost and swallowed up, this little fish retires into it in great security, and there sleeps, during which time the whale never stirs: but so soon as ever it goes out he immediately follows it; and if by accident he loses the sight of his little guide, he goes wandering here and there, and strikes his sides against the rocks like a ship that has lost her helm: which Plutarch affirms to have seen in the island of Anticyra.

Michel de Montaigne, *Apology for Raimond Sebond*, 1576

Sperm Wh[

The Whale

The biggest and the most monstrous creature in the Indish Ocean are the Whales called
Pristis and Balaena. These monstrous Whales named Balaenae, otherwhiles come into
our seas also. They say that in the coast of the Spanish Ocean by Gades, they are not
seen before midwinter when the daies be shortest: for at their set times they lie close in a
certaine calme deepe and large creeke, which they chuse to cast their spawne in, and there
delight above all places to breed. The Orcae, other monstrous fishes, know this full well,
and deadly enemies they bee unto the foresaid Whales. And verily, if I should pourtrait
them, I can resemble them to nothing els but a mightie masse and lumpe of flesh without
all fashion, armed with most terrible, sharpe, and cutting teeth. Well, these being ware
that the Whales are there, breake into this secret by-creeke out of the way, seeke them out,
and if they meet either with the young ones, or the dammes that have newly spawned, or
yet great with spawne, they all to cut & hacke them with their trenchant teeth; yea, they
run against them as it were a foist or ship of warre armed with sharpe brasen pikes in the

34

hery.

beake-head. But contrariwise, the Balaenes or Whales aforesaid, that cannot wind and turne aside for defence, and much lesse make head and resist, so unweldie as they bee by reason of their owne weightie and heavie bodie, (and as then either big bellied, or else weakened lately with the paines of travell and calving their young ones) have no other meanes of helpe and succour but to shoot them into the deepe, and gaine sea-roume to defend themselves from the enemie. On the other side, the Orcae labour (to cut them short of their purpose) to lie betweene them and home in their very way, and otherwhiles kill them unawares in the streights, or drive them upon the shelves and shallowes, or els force them against the very rockes, and so bruse them. When these combates and fights are seene, the sea seemeth as if it were angry with it selfe: for albeit no winds are up, but all calme in that creeke and gulfe, yet ye shall have waves in that place where they encounter (with the blasts of their breath, and the blowes given by the assailant) so great as no tempestuous whirlewinds whatsoever are not able to raise.

Pliny the Elder, *Naturalis Historia*, c.77

a Great Wonder at SEA

On the 19 of October 1645 being the Lord's Day, the good Shipp called The Bonaventuce of Weymouth, being bound for England, was bringing home her Merchandize from France, which was Wines, Linen-Cloth, and abundance of Walnuts: the day was very fair, and no winde stirring, so that the Ship for above three hours space lay hulling upon the Sea, being not able to move either one way or other, for want of winde, although shee was full Sayled and prepared to take the advantage of every Gale. Being put to some inconvenience by reason of this great Calme, the Sea-men for the present had nothing els to do but to look about them, many of them, as the miner is at Sea, wishing rather for a Tempest. Then being Wind-bound to stare about them and doe nothing, when behold not farre from them they saw a mighty rowling and working upon the water; and being amazed at the strangeness of the sight, they called unto one another, and were all come above Board, expecting what should occasion so strange a motion in the water, they found it to draw nearer to them, which made them the more eager to apprehend the cause, at length they perceived it to be a Whale, and that of no small proportion, but (as it were the Leviathan of the Sea) to transcend all other Whales in length and compasse. The Whale made towards the Shipp, which put the Marriners into a great fear, being not able to get from it, but they perceived the Monster of the Sea to come to them rather for refuge, then offence, for they saw it was followed by an infinite company of other Fish, as if all the fishes of the Sea were in

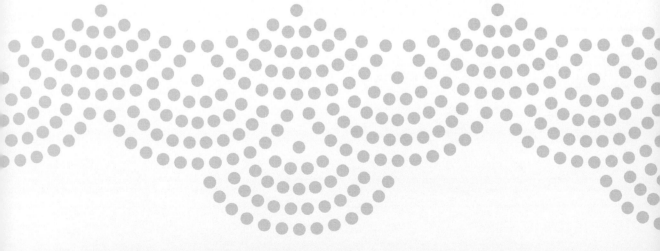

the pursuance of it … some of these fishes were in one shape, and some in another, but all most wonderfull to behold, who in great fury did use whatsoever weapons of offence that nature had afforded them to assault this Whale: nay, many of them were so eager in their fight, that they were seen to leap above the water, and as if they had gained an advantage of strength, they did throw themselves with greater rage against it, who being but one against so many thousands, was not able to withstand their fury, but making a most terrible crie, did what he could to come near the Ship. On this the amazed and distracted Sea-men, fearing the Whale should overturn their ship, and so drowne them all, discharged divers of their muskets against it, which it seemeth took effect, for presently they saw so great store of Blood that the sea was much coloured, and the Whale which before seemed to draw more near to the Ship for a safety, did now steer another course through the bloody and foaming waters. The infinite shoales of fish, which in incredible numbers did follow the Whale, were no way dismayed at the noise of the Muskets, nor at the fire which was given, but perceiving the wounded Whale to make away from the Ship, in greedy throng they pressed after it.

This made the Sea-men to wonder more, for many of them … having been often at Sea, never beheld the like thing before.

Perfect Relation of a Mighty Whale (pamphlet), 1645

THE ENORMOUS DIMENSIONS OF A <u>WHALE</u>

William Paley,
Natural Theology, 1819

The aorta of a whale is larger in the bore than the main pipe of the water-works at London Bridge; and the water roaring in its passage through that pipe, is inferior in impetus and velocity, to the blood gushing from the whale's heart. Hear D. Hunter's account of the dissection of a whale. 'The aorta measured a foot diameter. Ten or fifteen gallons of blood is thrown out of the heart at a stroke with an immense velocity, through a tube of a foot diameter. The whole idea fills the mind with wonder.'

ALL OF A BREACH AND FOAM

When we were off the Shoal-point I mention'd where we had but 20 Fathom-water, we had in the Night Abundance of Whales about the Ship, some a-head, others a-stern, and some on each side blowing and making a very dismal Noise; but when we came out again into deeper Water they left us. Indeed the Noise that they made by blowing and dashing of the Sea with their Tails, making it all of a Breach and Foam, was very dreadful to us, like the Breach of the Waves in very Shoal-water, or among Rocks. The Shoal these Whales were upon had Depth of Water sufficient, no less than 20 Fathom, as I said; and it lies in Lat. 22. deg. 22 min.

William Dampier, *A Voyage to New Holland,* 1698–99

Too Absurd
to be true

❧

I RECOLLECT WHEN A BOY VERY FREQUENTLY

HEARING OLD PEOPLE INTERRUPT A TOUGH

STORY WITH 'DARBY, DID YOU EVER SEE A WHALE?'

THEREBY INTIMATING THAT THE EXISTENCE OF

THAT ANIMAL, NOW SO COMMON AND WELL KNOWN,

WAS CONSIDERED TOO ABSURD AN IDEA TO BE

ENTITLED TO A PLACE IN A SERIOUS TREATISE

UPON ZOOLOGY.

❧

Nathaniel Ames, *Nautical Reminiscences*, 1832

ANATOMY OF A WHALE

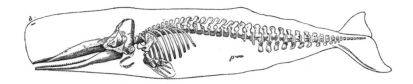

These spout-holes, or nostrils, in all the cetaceous tribe, have been already described: in this whale there are two, one on each side the head before the eyes, and crooked, somewhat like the holes on the belly of a violin. From these holes this animal blows the water very fiercely, and with such a noise, that it roars like a hollow wind, and may be heard at three miles' distance. When wounded, it then blows more fiercely than ever, so that it sounds like the roaring of the sea in a great storm …

Two great strong bones sustain the under lip, lying against each other in the shape of a half-moon: some of these are twenty feet long; they are seen in several gardens set up against each other, and are usually mistaken for the ribs of this animal.

As these animals resemble quadrupeds in conformation, so they bear a strong resemblance in some of their appetites and manners. The female joins with the male, as is asserted, *more humano*, and once in two years feels the accesses of desire …

Their fidelity to each other exceeds whatever we are told of even the constancy of birds. Some fishers, as Anderson informs us, having struck one of two whales, a male and a female, that were in company together, the wounded fish made a long and terrible resistance: it struck down a boat with three men in it, with a single blow of the tail, by which all went to the bottom. The other still attended its companion, and lent it every assistance; till, at last, the fish that was struck sunk under the number of its wounds; while its faithful associate, disdaining to survive the loss, with great bellowing stretched itself upon the dead fish, and shared its fate.

Oliver Goldsmith, *A History of the Earth and Animated Nature*, 1774

CLASH
of the
TITANS

At about eleven p.m. I was leaning over the lee rail, gazing steadily at the bright surface of the sea, where the intense radiance of the tropical moon made a broad path like a pavement of burnished silver. Eyes that saw not, mind only confusedly conscious of my surroundings, were mine; but suddenly I started to my feet with an exclamation, and stared with all my might at the strangest sight I ever saw. There was a violent commotion in the sea right where the moon's rays were concentrated, so great that, remembering our position, I was at first inclined to alarm all hands; for I had often heard of volcanic islands suddenly lifting their heads from the depths below, or disappearing in a moment, and, with Sumatra's chain of active volcanoes so near, I felt doubtful indeed of what was now happening. Getting the night-glasses out of the cabin scuttle, where they were always hung in readiness, I focussed them on the troubled spot, perfectly satisfied by a short examination that neither volcano nor earthquake had anything to do with what was going on; yet so vast were the forces engaged that I might well have been excused for my first supposition. A very large sperm whale was locked in deadly conflict with a cuttle-fish, or squid, almost as large as himself, whose interminable tentacles seemed to enlace the whole of his great body. The head of the whale

Charles Darwin sights a Whale

One day, off the East coast of Tierra del Fuego, we saw a grand sight in several spermaceti whales jumping upright quite out of the water, with the exception of their tail fins. As they fell down sideways, they splashed the water high up, and the sound reverberated like a distant broadside.

Charles Darwin, *The Voyage of the Beagle*, 1839

especially seemed a perfect net-work of writhing arms — naturally, I suppose, for it appeared as if the whale had the tail part of the mollusc in his jaws, and, in a business-like, methodical way, was sawing through it. By the side of the black columnar head of the whale appeared the head of the great squid, as awful an object as one could well imagine even in a fevered dream. Judging as carefully as possible, I estimated it to be at least as large as one of our pipes, which contained three hundred and fifty gallons; but it may have been, and probably was, a good deal larger. The eyes were very remarkable from their size and blackness, which, contrasted with the livid whiteness of the head, made their

appearance all the more striking. They were, at least, a foot in diameter, and, seen under such conditions, looked decidedly eerie and hobgoblin-like. All around the combatants were numerous sharks, like jackals round a lion, ready to share the feast, and apparently assisting in the destruction of the huge cephalopod. So the titanic struggle went on, in perfect silence as far as we were concerned, because, even had there been any noise, our distance from the scene of conflict would not have permitted us to hear it.

Frank T. Bullen, *The Cruise of the 'Cachalot'*, 1898

«Une baleine lançant de l'eau et un sanglier de mer»
D'après Gesnerus: Historiæ animalium lib. IV. 1558

MOTHER AND CALF

THE WHALE WAS SPORTING WITH ITS CALF IN THE BACKWATER OF A CURRENT. IT MIGHT HAVE BEEN THOUGHT TO BE GIVING IT A LESSON IN SWIMMING, BUT, ACTUALLY, LYING ON ITS SIDE, IT WAS PERMITTING THE LITTLE ONE TO RUB ITS BODY THE LENGTH OF ITS BREASTS. THE LITTLE THING, WHICH WAS UNABLE TO SEIZE ITS MOTHER'S NIPPLE IN ITS MOUTH, BY REASON OF HAVING ONLY A LOWER LIP, THE UPPER BEING A POINTED MUZZLE FURNISHED WITH EMBRYO BALEEN PLATES, OBEYED A NATURAL INSTINCT AND RUBBED ITS BODY AGAINST THE BREASTS OF ITS NURSE, IN ORDER TO CAUSE THE MILK TO SPURT FORTH. THIS MILK IS WHITE, THICK, AND OILY, AND DOES NOT MINGLE WITH SEA WATER, BUT FLOATS UPON IT. THE CALF ALLOWS IT TO ENTER ITS MOUTH WITH HALF A CASK OF WATER. THIS WATER IT EJECTS THROUGH ITS VENTS, WHILE GATHERING WITH ITS TONGUE AND SWALLOWING THE MILK WHICH HAS BECOME ENTANGLED BETWEEN THE HAIRS OF ITS BALEEN PLATES. WHAT AN ADMIRABLE METHOD OF SUCKLING! WHAT A MARVELLOUS USE OF ORGANS WHICH, AT FIRST SIGHT, APPEAR TO US SO IMPERFECT!

Dr Felix Maynard and Alexandre Dumas,
The Whalers, 1859

The social disposition
OF THE WHALE

November 13th: We are witnesses of a very remarkable exhibition of the social disposition of the whale. A week ago today, we passed several, and during the afternoon it was discovered that one of them continued to follow us, and was becoming more familiar, keeping under the ship and only coming out to breathe. A great deal of uneasiness was felt, lest in his careless gambols he might unship our rudder, or do us some other damage. It was said that bilge-water would drive him off, and the pumps were started, but to no purpose. At length more violent means were resorted to; volley after volley of rifle-shots were fired into him, billets of wood, bottles, etc., were thrown upon his head with such force as to separate the integument; to all of which he paid not the slightest attention, and he still continued to swim under us, keeping our exact rate of speed, whether in calm or storm, and rising to blow almost into the cabin windows. He seems determined to stay with us until he can find better company. His length is about eighty feet; his tail measures about twelve feet across; and in the calm, as we look down into the transparent water, we see him in all his huge proportions.

Charles M. Scammon, *The Marine Mammals of the North-western Coast of North America*, 1874

DÜRER AND THE WHALE

At Zierikzee in Zeeland a whale has been stranded by a high tide and a gale of wind. It is much more than 100 fathoms long and no man living in Zeeland has seen one even a third as long as this is. The fish cannot get off the land; the people would gladly see it gone, as they fear the great stink, for it is so large that they say it could not be cut in pieces and the blubber boiled down in half a year.

Albrecht Dürer, Antwerp, journal, 22 November–3 December 1520

THE *Infuriated* sperm whale

Mad with the agonies he endures from these fresh attacks, the infuriated Sperm Whale rolls over and over; he rears his enormous head, and with wide expanded jaws snaps at everything around him; he rushes at the boats with his head; they are propelled before him with vast swiftness, and sometimes utterly destroyed...

It is a matter of great astonishment that the consideration of the habits of so interesting, and, in a commercial point of view, of so important an animal (as the Sperm Whale) should have been so entirely neglected, or should have excited so little curiosity among the numerous, and many of them competent observers, that of late years, must have possessed the most abundant and most convenient opportunities of witnessing their habitudes.

Thomas Beale, *The Natural History of the Sperm Whale*, 1839

WHALE

Whale on the beach, you dinosaur,

what brought you smoothing into this dead harbor?

If you'd stayed inside you could have grown

as big as the Empire State. Still you are not a fish,

perhaps you like the land, you'd had enough of

holding your breath under water. What is it we want

of you? To take our warm blood into the great sea

and prove we are not the sufferers of God?

We are sick of babies crying and the birds flapping

loose in the air. We want the double to be big,

and ominous and we want to remember when you were

money in Massachusetts and yet were wild and rude

and killers. We want our killers dressed in black

like grease for we are sick of writing checks,

putting on our socks and working in the little boxes

we call the office.

∽

Anne Sexton, 'Whale', 1976

The Whale Skeleton

This information respecting the head was conveyed to the disconsolate curator, who was delighted at the discovery of his missing treasure. The head was still doomed to more troubles: the sharks had performed on their part a beneficial operation but the huge jaws, lying out of the water, had attracted some of those creatures (mischievous all over the world) called 'small boys', who were caught labouring hard at the lower jaw, endeavouring to extract the teeth; fortunately they were discovered before any material damage had been effected.

The men engaged, having now commenced cleaning the bones, began with the lower jaw, from its being a great attraction to depredators for the sake of the teeth. When this was completed, it was removed to the museum without the loss of a tooth. The preparation of the skeleton was proceeding with as much expedition as possible, and was nearly completed when one of the fins was missing, which, if not recovered, would have necessitated the replacement of it by artificial means, rendering the skeleton incomplete.

The disagreeable task of cleaning the huge bones of this animal, in a highly putrid state, occupied four days. It may be observed that when the men were about to tow the viscera to sea they were, fortunately, previously examined, when two separate bones were discovered, forming the os hyoides. From the quantity of oil still remaining in the bones, and the offensive smell emanating from them, they could not be removed, but were placed on one of the small islands in the harbour, where they remained for two months, under treatment with lime and other preparations, until they were properly bleached, when they were deposited in the museum.

Every part of the skeleton was now complete excepting one fin. One

The whale is a mammiferous animal without hind feet.

Baron Cuvier, *The Animal Kingdom*, 1817

morning the curator was informed that a strange fish was lying upon the rocks near the baths, at Woolloomooloo Bay. This, fortunately, was the lost fin, and was the more interesting from being the right one, the bones of which are considerably larger than the left, and more perfect. It was subsequently ascertained that the fin had been removed, for the oil, by the crew of a coasting vessel, while windbound in the bay but, a fair wind springing up, it was cut adrift and must have floated to the spot where it was found.

All obstacles being at length overcome, the skeleton was articulated in a masterly manner and became an object of great attraction to the public. The only parts deficient were two little, loose pelvic bones which, not being articulated to the rest, were likely to escape notice. But the curator now heard that another whale had been cast ashore on an open sandy beach between Port Hacking and Botany Bay. Although in an advanced stage of

decomposition, and in spite of the danger from the heavy seas which rolled upon the beach and dashed over the whale, he succeeded in getting into the carcass of the animal and, after repeated attempts, having been washed out several times by the heavy surf, in procuring the pelvic bones, which are found suspended in the soft parts.

The skeleton, when set up, was 33 feet 6 inches in its entire length; the length of the head from the snout to the occiput was 9 feet 6 inches. Although a complete skeleton of a sperm whale is rare in museums, the value of this specimen was much increased when it was found, on examination of its osteological structure, to be a new species. It has been named Catodon Australis; and a valuable account of it was published in Sydney by the distinguished naturalist, Mr W. S. McLeay.

George Bennett, c.1840

An indication of LAND

Most of the day calm, afterwards a little wind. Steered their course day and night, sailing less than thirteen leagues. In the morning found such abundance of weeds that the ocean seemed to be covered with them; they came from the west. Saw a pelican; the sea smooth as a river, and the finest air in the world. Saw a whale, an indication of land, as they always keep near the coast.

Christopher Columbus's journal, 21 September 1492

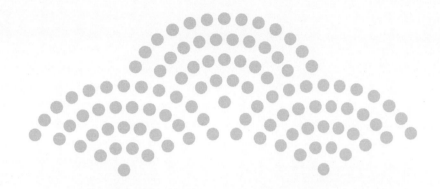

Spout and song

THE SPOUT'S CHARACTER CHANGED WITH WIND CONDITIONS. ON MOST OF THIS LEEWARD COAST, THE SPOUT WAS VERTICAL AND THE MIST HUNG IN THE AIR FOR A LONG TIME. ABOVE KAWAIHAI, THOUGH, WHERE THE TRADE WINDS VEERED OVER THE ISLANDS'S LOW NORTHERN TIP, THE BLOWS WERE BENT NEARLY HORIZONTAL AND THE MIST WAS QUICKLY ERASED. ON SOME DAYS WE SAW NO HUMPBACKS BUT HEARD THEIR VOICES. MEGAPTERA NOVAEANGLIAE OF ALL WHALES IS THE GREATEST SINGER. DR. ROGER PAYNE, FOREMOST STUDENT OF THIS SPECIES OF WHALE, BELIEVES THAT SOLITARY MALES DO THE SINGING. PAYNE HAS EVIDENCE THAT ALL THE HUMPBACKS BULLS OF A GIVEN REGION SING VARIATIONS ON THE SAME SONG, AND THAT THE SONG CHANGES EACH YEAR. BECAUSE WATER TRANSMITS SOUND SO WELL, AND BECAUSE THE HUMPBACK'S INSTRUMENT IS SO POWERFUL, THE SONGS CARRY TENS OF MILES, SOMETIMES HUNDREDS. IN THE PRISTINE OCEAN, BEFORE THE SEAS WERE POLLUTED BY PROPELLER SOUND, THE SINGING MUST HAVE CARRIED THOUSANDS OF MILES.

 ⁓

Kenneth Brower in Frank Stewart, *The Presence of Whales*, 1995

THE SIGNAL
HAS BEEN *Sounded*

It is known to seamen that a school of whales basking or sporting on the surface of the ocean, miles apart, with the convexity of the earth between them, will sometimes dive at the same instant — all gone out of sight in a moment. The signal has been sounded — too grave for the ear of the sailor at the masthead and his comrades on the deck — who nevertheless feel its vibrations in the ship as the stones of a cathedral are stirred by the bass of the organ.

Ambrose Bierce, *The Damned Thing*, 1894

Speed of the sperm whale

A sperm-whale could easily swim from Joppa to Alexandretta in three days and three nights; the distance is only about 300 miles. The cachalot swims, as a rule, at a rate of from 3 to 7 miles an hour, and just under the surface of the water. If a sperm-whale swam seven miles an hour, it might rest more than nine hours a day and still cover the distance from Joppa to Alexandretta in three days and three nights, i.e., 72 hours. If Jonah had travelled overland on horseback, it would have taken more than two weeks … The gait of the horse of Palestine is a brisk walk; they hardly ever trot.

Paul Haupt, 'Jonah's Whale', *Johns Hopkins University Circulars*, 1907

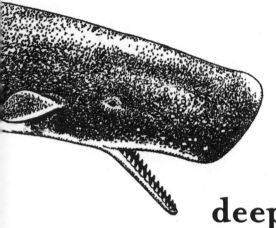

deep-sea *cephalopods*

In no department of zoological science, indeed, are we quite so much in the dark as with regard to the deep-sea cephalopods. A mere accident, for instance, it was that led to the Prince of Monaco's discovery of nearly a dozen new forms in the summer of 1895, a discovery in which the before-mentioned tentacle was included. It chanced that a cachalot was killed off Terceira by some sperm whalers, and in its last struggles charged almost to the Prince's yacht, missed it, rolled under, and died within twenty yards of his rudder. And in its agony it threw up a number of large objects, which the Prince, dimly perceiving they were strange and important, was, by a happy expedient, able to secure before they sank. He set his screws in motion, and kept them circling in the vortices thus created until a boat could be lowered. And these specimens were whole cephalopods and fragments of cephalopods, some of gigantic proportions, and almost all of them unknown to science!

H. G. Wells, *The Sea-Raiders*, 1896

Prelude to the Amber Whale

THOUGH IT LASH THE SHALLOWS THAT LINE THE BEACH,

AFAR FROM THE GREAT SEA-DEEPS,

THERE IS NEVER A STORM WHOSE MIGHT CAN REACH

WHERE THE VAST LEVIATHAN SLEEPS.

LIKE A MIGHTY THOUGHT IN A MIGHTY MIND

IN THE CLEAR COLD DEPTHS HE SWIMS;

WHILST ABOVE HIM THE PETTIEST FORM OF HIS KIND

WITH A DASH O'ER THE SURFACE SKIMS.

John Boyle O'Reilly,
'Prelude to the Amber Whale', 1873

A BREACHING WHALE

Their antics were amusing; they would first swim quietly, keeping their tails out of the water, and giving an occasional blow; then all of a sudden, one would raise his fins, two large pectoral fins, at least ten feet [3 m] in length, till they nearly met over his back, and would bring them down upon the water with a crash which covered him with foam and I almost fancied I could hear the blow at a distance of a mile; after that he would rear himself out of the water till little but his tail remained underneath, and then throw himself backwards into the air just like a rope dancer turning a summersault backwards.

Sir William Denison, Norfolk Island, September 1857

INCAPABLE *of noise*

One cannot help admiring the wonderful contrivance of Nature in constructing the Organs of these monstrous Animals so as to render them incapable of noise. Were they favour'd with the powers of Voice, who could stand the dreadful yelling that must be uttered when labouring under such a weight of pain.

Thomas Melville, *Journal of Voyages on* Britannia *and* Speedy, 1791–93

The breath of a whale

And the breath of the whale is frequently attended with such an insupportable foetor as to bring on a disorder in the brain. I therefore see no manner of difficulty in admitting that the breath of this serpent may be of that intoxicating quality attributed to it; and may be considered as an expedient for catching its prey, as otherwise the creature, from the flow movement of its body, would be utterly incapable of providing itself with food; whereas by this deleterious smell, the animal may be thrown into such horror and perplexity, as to be unable to move, but remain fixed like a statue, or faint away, whilst the snake gradually approaches and seizes it.

Antonio de Ulloa, *A Voyage to South-America*, 1758

BUBBLE Netting

The most spectacular feeding method is bubble netting. While this method is observed more frequently in the Northern Hemisphere, bubble netting has been observed in the Southern Hemisphere humpbacks. Diving below the krill swarm, humpbacks circle, blowing large bubbles about the size of a dinner plate. A glittering circle of bubbles ascends, acting as a trap, herding the krill into a smaller, denser mass. Two or even more animals may work this method, slowly spiralling upwards, creating the net of bubbles as they go. When the bubbles break the surface, completing the trap, the whales surge upwards through the krill, mouths wide open, jaws stretched to a stupendous size with water and krill. Once the lunge is completed, the whale closes its mouth, the large pleated throat remains expanded like a bellows, an enormous balloon of flesh extending from the top of the mouth down and out to nearly one-third of the animal's length. The process is repeated again and again, the whale taking tonnes of krill at a time.

Stephen Martin, *The Whale's Journey*, 2001

Voyage of the Kon-Tiki

The large shiny black forehead of the first whale was no more than two yards from us when it sank beneath the surface of the water, then we saw the huge blue-black bulk glide quietly under the raft right beneath our feet. It lay there for some time, dark and motionless, and we held our breath as we looked down on the gigantic curved back of a mammal a good deal longer than the raft.

Thor Heyerdahl, *Kon-Tiki*, 1950

In answer, it may be asked, why should not the early progenitors of the whales with baleen have possessed a mouth constructed something like the lamellated beak of a duck? Ducks, like whales, subsist by sifting the mud and water; and the family has sometimes been called Criblatores, or sifters.

Charles Darwin, *On the Origin of Species*, 1859

THE MOON BY WHALELIGHT

Whales glittered as they surfaced, and the moon seemed only their reflection. Close to shore, a right whale blew loudly. Another whale sneezed. The hydrophone picked up a stretched meow. No orcas were calling, but many right whales sighed and bleated through the pallid fog under the brilliant moon. Shivering, we decided to call it a night and returned to our tents and huts for a chilly sleep.

Diane Ackerman in Frank Stewart, *The Presence of Whales*, 1995

There go the ships: there is that Leviathan whom thou hast made to play therein.

Psalm 104:26

Suddenly a mighty mass emerged from the water, and shot up perpendicularly into the air. It was the whale.

Joseph C. Hart, *Miriam Coffin or the Whale-fishermen*, 1872

Inside a baleen whale's mouth

I could not stay up but a few minutes, it rained so very hard. My Husband wanted me to walk into the whale's mouth. He pushed me in a little ways, so I think I can say that I have been inside of a whale's mouth. Six or eight people could easily go in and sit down at one time. I would not hesitate about going in and sitting down if it was clean, but it was very wet and dirty from the rain. One cannot imagine without seeing it, how the mouth looks. Those long slabs of bone, set as thick together in the jaw as they can be — two rows of them — are like two rows of teeth though nothing like them in looks. I should say that the longest of these slabs was about six feet, but they tell me it is not at all uncommon to see them 15 or 20 feet long. These grow gradually shorter all the way from the back of the head to the entrance of the mouth, being quite short there — not more than two or three inches — and the hair very thick and white. All the rest, the whole length of the slabs, have hair on the edge, making the whole of the mouth lined with hair. It is black, the color of the bone, only that close to the roof or where the bone sets into the jaw. I could not imagine for what purpose this hair was, till my Husband explained to me. It seems that their food floats in masses, literally covering the water in spots. It is a fine substance, about as big as mustard seed, and surrounded by a gluey substance. This food floats on the top of the water. The whale moves along with his mouth open and draws in large quantities of it and it is strained through this hair. It seems singular that such fine food should have been formed for so large a fish. These fish are truly one of the wonderful works of God and well may we think that everything in the deep is wonderful.

The journal of Eliza Williams on board the *Florida*, 1858–61

Chapter 2

AND GOD CREATED
great WHALES

Mythologising the whale

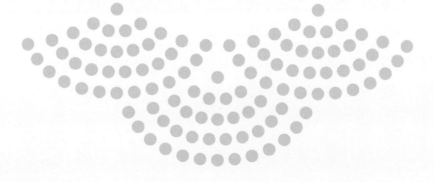

JONAS.

It is no surprise that the majestic and mysterious whale has inspired myth and legend in cultures from virtually every corner of the globe. In Western society, one of the best known stories is that of *Jonah and the Whale*, where the Galilean Jonah is swallowed by a whale and lives in its belly for three days and three nights before being set free to preach God's word. The whale, with its huge girth and gaping mouth, is generally portrayed as a fearsome beast in legends, as in a tale from *One Thousand and One Nights*, where Sinbad and his sailors land on what they think is an island, later to discover in terror — when it shakes them off — that it is in fact a whale. However, the whale is sometimes a martyr to its huge size, being easily stranded in shallow water, and at the mercy of humans, as in the Maori lengend *Tinirau and His Pet Whale*. In the mythology of some cultures the whale is a mystical being, or an object of worship, such as in China where the god of the sea is said to have once been a whale.

And behold, the call was answered. A huge black shining shape broke water but a short distance out in the bay, a great sperm whale. From its spiracle it blew a geyser-spout of vapour with the hissing roar of one of those steam pipes on Whakaari. A little rainbow arched its head, in the misty spray of the spout jet. It raised its powerful tail and swept the flukes down and beat the water with a noise that could have been heard a mile away. The sea boiled about it with the commotion of its mighty salute to the magician who stood on the cliff-top.

The Wizard Who Was Marooned, Maori folktale

tis primo notat aratus græce. Cicero nodū cæleſtē di
cit:qui utrūcʒ uolunt ſignificare:eū nodū nō ſolū piſciū: ſed ét
totius ſphæræ eſſe:quo enim loco é circulus ab arietis pede Me
ſembrinos dicit:qui meridé ſignificet.& quo loco is circulus me
ſembrinos coniungitur:& tranſit æquinoctialé circulū : in ipſa
coniūctione circulorum nodus p ſciū ſignificat:quia eū nō mo
do nodū piſcium ſed etiam cæleſtium nodum appellauernnt.

Iſtrix a media cauda diuiditur ab hyemali circulo
ſpectans ad exortus:roſtro ppe poſteriore arietis pe
dem iungens:huius priore parté corporis:quæ ſpe
ctat ad exortus prope alluere flumen Eridani uide
tur.Hæc cadit exorto cancro & leone:exoritur aūt
cū centauro & geminis.ſed habet i extrema cauda ſtellas duas
obſcuras.Ab eo loco uſcʒ ad reliqui corpor s curuaturam quin
cʒ. Sub uentre ſex.Omnino ſunt tredecim .

iouas

T factum e vbm

JONAH

CHAPTER I

Now the word of the LORD came unto Jonah the son of Amittai, saying, Arise, go to Nineveh, that great city, and cry against it; for their wickedness is come up before me. But Jonah rose up to flee unto Tarshish from the presence of the LORD, and went down to Joppa; and he found a ship going to Tarshish: so he paid the fare thereof, and went down into it, to go with them unto Tarshish from the presence of the LORD. But the LORD sent out a great wind into the sea, and there was a mighty tempest in the sea, so that the ship was like to be broken. Then the mariners were afraid, and cried every man unto his god, and cast forth the wares that were in the ship into the sea, to lighten it of them. But Jonah was gone down into the sides of the ship; and he lay, and was fast asleep. So the shipmaster came to him, and said unto him, What meanest thou, O sleeper? arise, call upon thy God, if so be that God will think upon us, that we perish not. And they said every one to his fellow, Come, and let us cast lots, that we may know for whose cause this evil is upon us. So they cast lots, and the lot fell upon Jonah. Then said they unto him, Tell us, we pray thee, for whose cause this evil is upon us; What is thine occupation? and whence comest thou? what is thy country? and of what people art thou? And he said unto them, I am an Hebrew; and I fear the LORD, the God of heaven, which hath made the sea and the dry land. Then were the men exceedingly afraid, and said unto him. Why hast thou done this? For the men knew that he fled from the presence of the LORD, because he had told them. Then said they unto him, What shall we do unto thee, that the sea may be calm unto us? for the sea wrought, and was tempestuous. And he said unto them, Take me up, and cast me forth into the sea; so shall the sea be calm unto you: for I know

BOOK 32: Jonah

that for my sake this great tempest is upon you. Nevertheless the men rowed hard to bring it to the land; but they could not: for the sea wrought, and was tempestuous against them. Wherefore they cried unto the LORD, and said, We beseech thee, O LORD, we beseech thee, let us not perish for this man's life, and lay not upon us innocent blood: for thou, O LORD, hast done as it pleased thee. So they look up Jonah, and cast him forth into the sea: and the sea ceased from her raging. Then the men feared the LORD exceedingly, and offered a sacrifice unto the LORD, and made vows. Now the LORD had prepared a great fish to swallow up Jonah. And Jonah was in the belly of the fish three days and three nights.

CHAPTER II

Then Jonah prayed unto the LORD his God out of the fish's belly, And said, I cried by reason of mine affliction unto the LORD, and he heard me; out of the belly of hell cried I, and thou heardest my voice.

For thou hadst cast me into the deep, in the midst of the seas; and the floods compassed me about: all thy billows and thy waves passed over me. Then I said, I am cast out of thy sight; yet I will look again toward thy holy temple. The waters compassed me about, even to the soul: the depth closed me round about, the weeds were wrapped about my head. I went down to the bottoms of the mountains; the earth with her bars was about me for ever: yet hast thou brought up my life from corruption, O LORD my God. When my soul fainted within me I remembered the LORD: and my prayer came in unto thee, into thine holy temple. They that observe lying vanities forsake their own mercy. But I will sacrifice unto thee with the voice of thanksgiving; I will pay that that I have vowed. Salvation is of the LORD. And the LORD spake unto the fish, and it vomited out Jonah upon the dry land.

SINBAD AND THE WHALE

'The First Voyage of Sinbad', *One Thousand and One Nights*, AD 800–900

In our voyage we touched at several islands, where we sold or exchanged our goods. One day, whilst under sail, we were becalmed near a little island, almost even with the surface of the water, which resembled a green meadow. The captain ordered his sails to be furled, and permitted such persons as had a mind to do so to land upon the island, amongst whom I was one.

But while we were diverting ourselves with eating and drinking, and recovering ourselves from the fatigue of the sea, the island on a sudden trembled, and shook us terribly.

They perceived the trembling of the island on board the ship, and called us to re-embark speedily, or we should all be lost, for what we took for an island was only the back of a whale. The nimblest got into the sloop, others betook themselves to swimming; but for my part I was still upon the back of the whale when he dived into the sea, and had time only to catch hold of a piece of wood that we had brought out of the ship to make a fire. Meanwhile, the captain, having received those on board who were in the sloop, and taken up some of those that swam, resolved to use the favourable gale that had just risen, and hoisting his sails, pursued his voyage, so that it was impossible for me to regain the ship.

Thorhall's *Reward*

Saga of Eric the Red, 14th century Norse legend

Pl. LXXXIII. — MAMMIFÈRES MONODELPHES. — CÉTACÉS

Baleine franche ou boréale (*Balæna mysticetus*).

ANIMAUX VERTÉBRÉS. — MAMMIFÈRES.

657

They stayed there that winter, which turned out to be a very severe one; they had made no provision for it during the summer, and now they ran short of food and the hunting failed. They moved out to the island (Straum Island) in hope of finding game, or stranded whales, but there was little food to be found there … Then they prayed to God to send them something to eat, but the response was not as prompt as they would have liked.

Meanwhile Thorhall the Hunter disappeared and they went out to search for him. They searched for three days; and on the fourth day Karlsefni and Bjarni found him on top of a cliff. He was staring up at the sky with eyes and mouth and nostrils agape, scratching himself and pinching himself and mumbling. They asked him what he was doing there; he replied that it was no concern of theirs … They urged him to come back home with them and he did.

A little later a whale was washed up and they rushed to cut it up. No one recognized what kind of a whale it was, not even Karlsefni, who was an expert on whales. The cooks boiled the meat, but when it was eaten it made them all ill.

Then Thorhall the Hunter walked over and said, 'Has not Redbeard [Thor] turned out to be more successful than your Christ? This was my reward for the poem I composed in honor of my patron, Thor; he has seldom failed me.' When the others realized this they refused to use the whalemeat and threw it over a cliff, and committed themselves to God's mercy.

KING OLAF TRYGGVASON'S *Saga*

King Harald sends a Warlock in a transformed Shape to Iceland. — King Harald told a warlock to hie to Iceland in some altered shape, and to try what he could learn there to tell him: and he set out in the shape of a whale. And when he came near to the land he went to the west side of Iceland, north around the land, where he saw all the mountains and hills full of land-serpents, some great, some small. When he came to Vapnafjord he went in towards the land, intending to go on shore; but a huge dragon rushed down the dale against him with a train of serpents, paddocks, and toads, that blew poison towards him. Then he turned to go westward around the land as far as Eyafjord, and he went into the fjord. Then a bird flew against him, which was so great that its wings stretched over the mountains on either side of the fjord, and many birds, great and small, with it. Then he swam farther west, and then south into Breidefjord. When he came into the fjord a large grey bull ran against him, wading into the sea, and bellowing fearfully, and he was followed by a crowd of land-serpents. From thence he went round by Reikaness, and wanted to land at Vikarskeid, but there came down a hill-giant against him with an iron staff in his hands. He was a head higher than the mountains, and many other giants followed him. He then swam eastward along the land, and there was nothing to see, he said, but sand and vast deserts, and, without the skerries, high-breaking surf; and the ocean between the countries was so wide that a long-ship could not cross it. At that time Brod-helge dwelt in Vapnafjord, Eyolf Valgerdson in Eyafjord, Thord Gelle in Breidefjord, and Thorodd gode in Olfus. Then the Danish king turned about with his fleet, and sailed back to Denmark.

Hakon the earl settled habitations again in the country that had been laid waste, and paid no scatt as long as he lived to Denmark.

The Olaf Sagas, 12th—13th century Norse legend

No. 53. CETUS.

In Chinese mythology there are references to 'moonlight pearls' that come from the eyes of female whales.

KUN

...

YU QIANG, LEGITIMATE GRANDSON OF
GOD THE SUPREME, WAS THE GOD OF SEA
AND ALSO THE GOD OF WIND IN THE NORTH
SEA. WHEN HE APPEARED AS THE GOD
OF SEA, HE WAS HUMAN-FACED AND FISH-
BODIED WITH HANDS AND FEET; WHEN HE
WAS IN THE CAPACITY OF THE WIND GOD,
HE WAS HUMAN-FACED AND BIRD-BODIED.
WHY, THEN, WAS HE NOW FISH-BODIED,
NOW BIRD-BODIED? IN FACT, HE WAS ONCE
AN ENORMOUS FISH CALLED KUN RESIDING
IN THE NORTH SEA, A WHALE AS A MATTER
OF FACT, AS LARGE AS SEVERAL
THOUSAND LI IN SIZE.

...

The Five Divine Mountains of
Guixu and the Giants of the Dragon Kingdom,
Chinese myth

Sharing the Whale

The Saga of Grettir the Strong

One summer Thorgils Maksson found a whale at the Almenningar and went out at once with his men to cut it up. When the two foster-brothers heard of it they went there too, and at first it seemed as if matters would be settled peaceably. Thorgils proposed that they should share equally that part of the whale which was yet uncut, but they wanted to have all the uncut part or else to share the entire whale. Thorgils positively refused to give up any portion of what had already been cut. They began to use threats and at last took to their arms and fought. Thorgeir and Thorgils fought each of them desperately together without either prevailing. After a long and furious battle Thorgils fell slain by Thorgeir. In another place Thormod was fighting with the followers of Thorgils, and he overcame them, killing three. Those who remained of Thorgils' party went off after he fell to Midfjord, taking his body with them and feeling that they had suffered a great loss. The foster-brothers took possession of the whole whale. The affair is referred to in the memorial poem which Thormod composed upon Thorgeir.

Origin of the Killer Whale

John R. Swanton

Tlingit Myths and Texts, 1909

A MAN NAMED NATSIHLANE,
belonging to the Tsague'dî (Seal people),
made killer whales. He first tried to carve
them out of red cedar, then out of hemlock,
then out of all other kinds of wood in
succession. He took each set of figures to the
beach and tried to make them swim out, but
instead they floated up on the surface. Last of
all he tried yellow cedar, and was successful.

He made these of different sorts. On one
he marked white lines with Indian chalk from
the corners of its mouth back to its head. He
said, 'This is going to be the white-mouthed
killer whale'. When he first put them into the
water he headed them up the inlet, telling
them that whenever they went up to the heads
of the bays they were to hunt for seal, halibut,
and all other things under the sea; but he told
them not to hurt a human being. When you
are going up the bay, people will say to you,
'Give us something to eat'. Before this people
did not know what the killer whale is.

***

Another thing people did not know was that
the killer whale could go ashore and camp.
One time a man married a high-caste woman
and went up to the head of a certain bay with
her, because he knew that the killer whales
always went there. On the way they saw a camp
fire blazing upon the shore. There were killer
whales encamped here, but he thought they
were human beings and landed to see them.
When they got close in, he jumped into the
water to urinate. All at once the killer-whale
chief said, 'I feel people's looks. Go outside
and look on the beach.' But, when they saw
him urinating, they started off, leaving their
camp just as it was, jumped into the water,
and swam away.

Then he went up to the camp with his
wife, and they saw all kinds of food there.
His wife said, 'It is lucky that we came across
this'; and after awhile the man said, 'Let us
cook some, my wife'. Then the woman took
her cooking basket and put some water into
it. Presently she said, 'Way out there is a
canoe coming'. It was a black canoe. She

said, 'We better leave this alone until the canoe comes so that we can invite them to eat with us'. Her husband said, 'All right'. By and by his wife said, 'What is the matter? To my eyes it does not appear like a canoe. It is too black.' It was really a young killer whale, under which the other killer whales were swimming to make it appear like a canoe. When the supposed canoe reached land, the whales rushed ashore, seized the woman, who had concealed herself behind her husband, and carried her down to the sea. They took her away because her husband had taken their provisions. This time, when the killer whales rose again, instead of appearing like only one canoe, they came up out of the water thick everywhere and began to swim down the bay very fast. Meanwhile the husband went down to his canoe, got in, and paddled after them along the shore. But, when they came to a high cliff where the water went down deep, all the whales suddenly dived out of sight.

Now the man climbed to the top of this cliff, fastened a bough to his head and another slim spruce bough around his waist, filled the space inside of his shirt with rocks, and jumped into the ocean at the spot where his wife had disappeared, falling upon a smooth, mossy place on the bottom. When he awoke, he arose, looked about, and saw a long town near by. He entered the last house, which proved to belong to the chief of the shark people.

In this house he saw a man with a crooked mouth peeping out at him from behind a post. A long time before, when he had been fishing, a shark had cut his line and carried off the hook, and it was this hook that now peeped out at him. It said, 'Master, it is I. When your line broke, they took me down here and have made me a slave.'

Then he said to the shark chief, 'Is there any news in this town?' and he replied, 'Nothing especial in our town, but right across from us is the killer-whales' town, and recently we heard that a woman had been captured there and is now married to the killer whale chief'. Then the shark chief continued: 'The killer-whale chief has a slave, who is always chopping wood back in the forest with a stone ax. When you come to him, say within yourself, "I wish your stone ax would break". Wish it continually.' So the shark instructed him.

Then he went over to the killer-whale town, and, when the slave's ax did break, he went up to him and said, 'I will help you to fix that stone ax if you will tell me where my wife is'. So he began to fix it in place for him. It was the only stone ax in the killer-whale tribe. Then the slave said, 'I always bring wood down and make a fire in the evening, after which my master sends me for water. When you see me going after water, come to the door and wait there for me. As soon as I come in I am going to push over the fire. At the same time I am going to empty the water into it so as to make a quantity of steam. Then rush in and carry out your wife.'

The man followed these directions and started away with his wife. Then his halibut hook shouted, 'This way, my master, this way'. So he ran toward the shark people's town, and they pursued him. Now the killer whales attacked the shark people because they said that the sharks had instructed him what to do, and they killed many sharks.

In return the sharks began to make themselves strong. They were going out again to fight the killer whales. They went to some rocks and began sharpening their teeth. Then they began the battle, and whenever the killer whales approached, the sharks would run against their bellies and rip them open, letting out their entrails. The whole bay was full of killer whales and sharks. What happened to the woman is not told.

نذناه بالعرا وهو سقيم وانشا عليـة

سغلى م

فعاب

صدره

لبس الش

من ذلك

الى نينو

رجع اليـ

با دمير

وهـل

والمآ ب

وة

فلولا انه كان من المسبحين للبث في بطنه الى يوم يبعثو

عالى

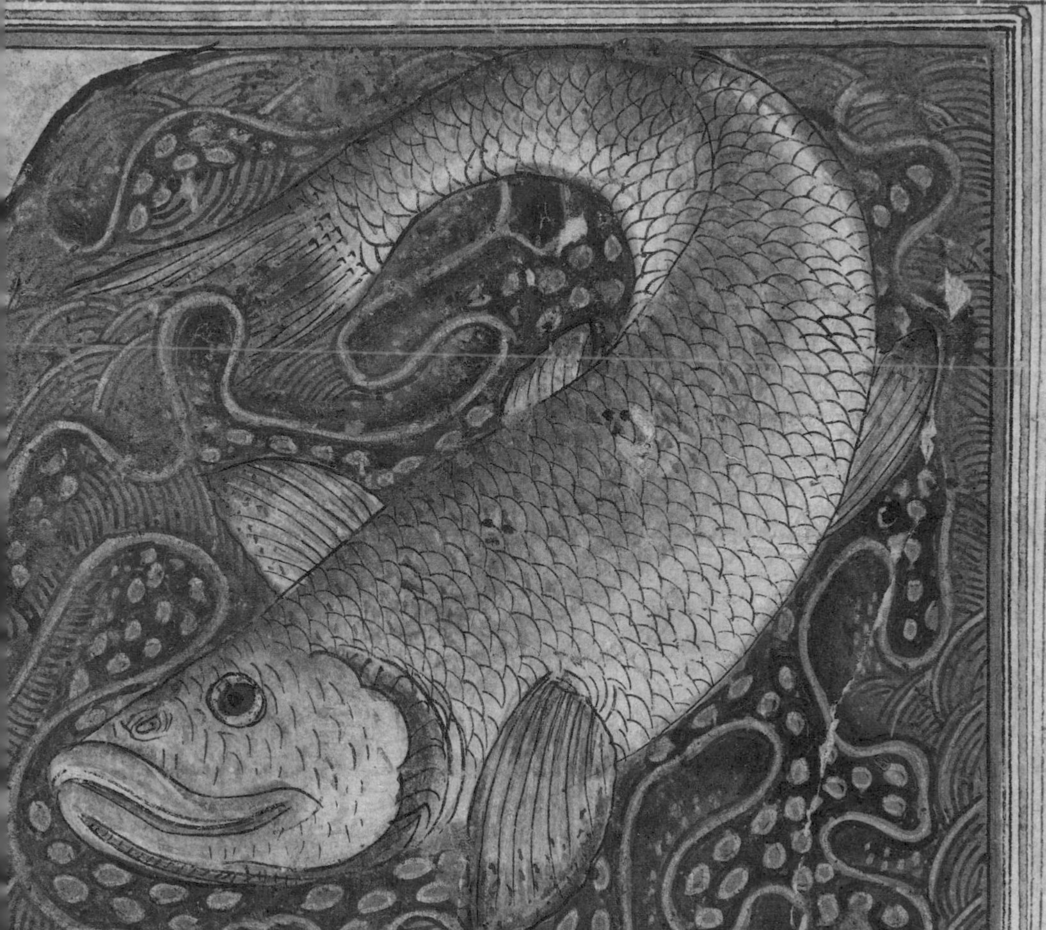

كان

الشجره

ساق

على

ك

ق صدر

اجعته

لهم فلما

واعلبه

مختلفة

ه المرج

قصة

Neptunu eiunt poetaru fabule Amphitae voluisse iconiugiū accepe que cū obuerecundis
magnitudine et urgi tuitatis obseruātiā Adathlante confugisse neptunus postea
itū reteros missos . . delphinū etiam dicitur misisse. Qui padthlanus insulas circuuagans.
eam Adloci . . . tus sit. Et neptuno inmatrimoniū Adsūndam adduxent. exobhanc
. . . clusam inter astra collocatus. Habet stellas inore . i. incornu . ii. inuentris
pennulis . ii. indorso . i. incauda . ii. sunt omnes . viiii.

Tam magni curuus capricornu corpora pprei
Delphini iacet . haut nimio lustratus nitore
Pixcet quadruplicis stellas infronte locatas
Quas interuallum binas disterminat unum
Cetera pars latet et nullo cum lumine serpit
Ille que fulgent luces exore corusco
Sunt inter partes gelidas Aquilonis locatas
Atque interspatium eclaea uestigia solis
At pars inferior delphini fusa uidetur
Intersolis iter simul inter flamina uenta
Umb: erumpit quad summu sp̄s austri

Fair, Brown, and Trembling

Celtic folktale

It happened, when the two sisters were walking by the seashore, that a little cowboy was down by the water minding cattle, and saw Fair push Trembling into the sea; and next day, when the tide came in, he saw the whale swim up and throw her out on the sand. When she was on the sand she said to the cowboy: 'When you go home in the evening with the cows, tell the master that my sister Fair pushed me into the sea yesterday; that a whale swallowed me, and then threw me out, but will come again and swallow me with the coming of the next tide; then he'll go out with the tide, and come again with tomorrow's tide, and throw me again on the strand. The whale will cast me out three times. I'm under the enchantment of this whale, and cannot leave the beach or escape myself. Unless my husband saves me before I'm swallowed the fourth time, I shall be lost. He must come and shoot the whale with a silver bullet when he turns on the broad of his back. Under the breast-fin of the whale is a reddish-brown spot. My husband must hit him in that spot, for it is the only place in which he can be killed.'

When the cowboy got home, the eldest sister gave him a draught of oblivion, and he did not tell.

Next day he went again to the sea. The whale came and cast Trembling on shore again. She asked the boy: 'Did you tell the master what I told you to tell him?'

'I did not,' said he; 'I forgot.'

'How did you forget?' asked she.

'The woman of the house gave me a drink that made me forget.'

'Well, don't forget telling him this night; and if she gives you a drink, don't take it from her.'

As soon as the cowboy came home, the eldest sister offered him a drink. He refused to take it till he had delivered his message and told all to the master. The third day the prince went down with his gun and a silver bullet in it. He was not long down when the whale came and threw Trembling upon the beach as the two days before. She had no power to speak to her husband till he had killed the whale. Then the whale went out, turned over once on the broad of his back, and showed the spot for a moment only. That moment the prince fired. He had but the one chance, and a short one at that; but he took it, and hit the spot, and the whale, mad with pain, made the sea all around red with blood, and died.

That minute Trembling was able to speak, and went home with her husband, who sent word to her father what the eldest sister had done. The father came, and told him any death he chose to give her to give it. The prince told the father he would leave her life and death with himself. The father had her put out then on the sea in a barrel, with provisions in it for seven years.

And God created great whales.

Genesis, I:2I

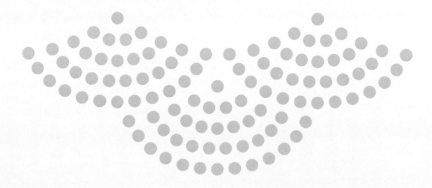

The Idol and the Whale

JAPANESE FOLKTALE

Mr Shark was off. Arriving in that part of the Northern Sea where the Whale was blowing, he told his story. All the reports of the idol's size were true and the circumference of its pedestal was five thousand feet.

Frantic with jealousy and unable to believe the story, the Whale determined to see for himself. Putting on his magic boots, which enabled him to travel overland, he reached the temple at Kamakura at night, when all men were abed, and knocked at the door.

'Come in,' sounded the Buddha's voice like the boom of a bell.

'I cannot,' groaned the Whale.

'Why not?'

'Because I am far too large.'

'Who are you?'

'I am the great white Whale of the Northern Sea.'

'What do you want?'

'I want to see if you are bigger than I am. I cannot get in to you, so please come out to me.' Thus respectfully addressed, the idol stepped off his pedestal, and presented himself outside. The Whale was so overpowered that he trembled and knocked his head on the earth in profound respect. He now believed that what he had heard was almost true. On the other hand, the Buddha was astounded at the Whale's prodigious bulk.

By this time the chief priest and guardian of the temple was awake and up. He was nearly frightened out of his senses to find the pedestal empty. But hearing the conversation, and being invited by both the idol and the Whale to take their measure, he seized his rosary and began to measure. Each watched the other with a jealous eye, but the Whale, to his intense satisfaction, found that he was two inches longer and taller than his rival.

That settled it. Without even once thanking the idol or the priest for the trouble he had given them, he flippered off, slid into the water and was soon spouting in triumph in the great Northern Sea. The idol quietly returned to his pedestal, and as for the priest, when he told his story next day, both his brethren and the people declared it must have been a dream.

Nevertheless the man in the dry-goods store and the dealer in wood and iron settled their own long standing quarrel as to what was a foot and agreed to differ. To this day the 'whale foot' is two inches longer than the 'metal foot'.

PERSEUS *and the* WHALE

Charles Kingsley, *The Heroes,* 1899

And Perseus feared to go inland, but flew along the shore above the sea; and he went on all the day, and the sky was black with smoke; and he went on all the night, and the sky was red with flame.

And at the dawn of day he looked toward the cliffs; and at the water's edge, under a black rock, he saw a white image stand ...

So he came near; but when he came, it was no statue, but a maiden of flesh and blood; for he could see her tresses streaming in the breeze; and as he came closer still, he could see how she shrank and shivered when the waves sprinkled her with cold salt spray. Her arms were spread above her head, and fastened to the rock with chains of brass ...

'Do not fear me, fair one; I am a Hellen, and no barbarian. What cruel men have bound you? But first I will set you free.'

And he tore at the fetters, but they were too strong for him; while the maiden cried —

'Touch me not; I am accursed, devoted as a victim to the sea-Gods. They will slay you, if you dare to set me free.'

'Let them try,' said Perseus; and drawing Herpé from his thigh, he cut through the brass as if it had been flax ...

And she answered, weeping —

'I am the daughter of Cepheus, King of Iopa, and my mother is Cassiopoeia of the beautiful tresses, and they called me Andromeda, as long as life was mine. And I stand bound here, hapless that I am, for the sea-monster's food, to atone for my mother's sin. For she boasted of me once that I was fairer than Atergatis, Queen of the Fishes; so she in her wrath sent the sea-floods, and her brother the Fire King sent the earthquakes, and wasted all the land, and after the floods a monster bred of the slime, who devours all living things. And now he must devour me, guiltless though I am — me who never harmed a living thing, nor saw a fish upon the shore but I gave it life, and threw it back into the sea; for in our land we eat no fish, for fear of Atergatis their queen. Yet the priests say that nothing but my blood can atone for a sin which I never committed.'

But Perseus laughed, and said, 'A sea-monster? I have fought with worse than him:

I would have faced Immortals for your sake; how much more a beast of the sea?'

Then Andromeda looked up at him, and new hope was kindled in her breast, so proud and fair did he stand, with one hand round her, and in the other the glittering sword. But she only sighed, and wept the more, and cried ...

'There he comes, with the sunrise, as they promised. I must die now. How shall I endure it? Oh, go! Is it not dreadful enough to be torn piecemeal, without having you to look on?' And she tried to thrust him away ...

On came the great sea-monster, coasting along like a huge black galley, lazily breasting the ripple, and stopping at times by creek or headland to watch for the laughter of girls at their bleaching, or cattle pawing on the sand-hills, or boys bathing on the beach. His great sides were fringed with clustering shells and sea-weeds, and the water gurgled in and out of his wide jaws, as he rolled along, dripping and glistening in the beams of the morning sun.

At last he saw Andromeda, and shot forward to take his prey, while the waves foamed white behind him, and before him the fish fled leaping.

Then down from the height of the air fell Perseus like a shooting star; down to the crests of the waves, while Andromeda hid her face as he shouted; and then there was silence for a while.

At last she looked up trembling, and saw Perseus springing toward her; and instead of the monster a long black rock, with the sea rippling quietly round it.

Who then so proud as Perseus, as he leapt back to the rock, and lifted his fair Andromeda in his arms, and flew with her to the cliff-top, as a falcon carries a dove?

Who so proud as Perseus, and who so joyful as all the Aethiop people? For they had stood watching the monster from the cliffs, wailing for the maiden's fate. And already a messenger had gone to Cepheus and Cassiopoeia, where they sat in sackcloth and ashes on the ground, in the innermost palace chambers, awaiting their daughter's end. And they came, and all the city with them, to see the wonder, with songs and with dances, with cymbals and harps, and received their daughter back again, as one alive from the dead.

HARD WERE THE BLOWS
WHICH WERE DEALT AT RIFSKER;
NO WEAPONS THEY HAD BUT
STEAKS OF THE WHALE.
THEY BELABOURED EACH OTHER
WITH ROTTEN BLUBBER.
UNSEEMLY METHINKS IS SUCH
WARFARE FOR MEN.

The Saga of Grettir the Strong, 14th-century Icelandic legend

King Sulemani and the Whale

Proud King Sulemani prayed to God to give him the power to be able to feed not only his own kingdom's subjects and animals but all the creatures on earth. God thought this was a foolish request and decided to teach King Sulemani a lesson. From the very bottom of the ocean God raised a giant whale, mightier than any whale ever seen before; almost the size of a mountain. The whale had a huge appetite, and as soon as he arrived on land in Sulemani's kingdom he began to eat. And he ate and ate until there wasn't a grain of food left in the land. When all the food was gone, the whale roared at King Sulemani to feed him. The terrified and desperate king asked the whale if there were any more creatures like him under the sea. The whale replied to the king's horror that there were seventy thousand more in his tribe, just as huge and hungry as himself. On hearing these words the king realised the impossibility of feeding all of earth's creatures himself, and prostrated himself to God and begged his forgiveness for his stupid request.

EAST AFRICAN LEGEND

The Whale Man and His Canoe

AUSTRALIAN ABORIGINAL LEGEND

Back in the dreaming, when the world was young, ice melted. The water levels rose and some of the land began to disappear. All the animals wanted to escape to the other side, but no one had a canoe big enough to carry them, except the Whale Man.

The Whale Man was a big fella and he had a huge canoe, but he wouldn't loan his canoe to anyone. So the animals all met and decided to try to get hold of the Whale Man's canoe. That way they could go across the waters to reach the land on the other side before it was too late.

So it was arranged. One day, when the Whale Man was walking down the beach, dragging his canoe behind him along the water's edge, the Starfish Man approached him. 'Hey brother!' he said. 'I see some sea lice on your head. Why don't you come over here to these rocks where I'm sitting and put your head in my lap. I'll scratch and get rid of some of them and make you feel good.'

The Whale Man agreed to do this, but because he loved his canoe, he hung on tightly to the bark rope.

The Starfish Man scratched around Whale Man's ears and made him feel good for a little while. When he was doing this and the Whale Man was preoccupied, the Koala Man sneaked up behind them and cut the bark rope with his knife. He quietly pushed the canoe away and all the other creatures silently crept into the boat. Then they gently pushed it into the water and began to paddle off, as quickly as they could. The Koala Man did all the paddling, which developed the muscles on his arms and made them very strong.

THE DOLPHINS, THE WHALES *and* THE SPRAT

The Dolphins quarrelled with the Whales, and before very long they began fighting with one another. The battle was very fierce, and had lasted some time without any sign of coming to an end, when a Sprat thought that perhaps he could stop it; so he stepped in and tried to persuade them to give up fighting and make friends. But one of the Dolphins said to him contemptuously, 'We would rather go on fighting till we're all killed than be reconciled by a Sprat like you!'
Aesop (620–560 BC)

Meanwhile, every so often the Whale Man asked, 'How's my canoe there, brother?'

With one hand scratching the Whale Man's head, the Starfish Man tapped a piece of wood onto the side of the rock they were sitting on with the other hand. 'See, that's your canoe.' This was repeated a few times, but somehow it didn't sound right.

Sensing that something was wrong, the Whale Man suddenly jumped to his feet. He looked across the waters to see his beloved canoe disappearing over the horizon, and realised he'd been tricked.

This deception made the Whale Man extremely angry. He struck the Starfish Man, who managed to counter with one tremendous blow. The force of the impact opened a hole in the Whale Man's head, but Whale Man was very powerful. He pounded the Starfish Man until he fell senseless onto a rock, from which he slid onto the sand. There he lies to this day, all squashed out in the water.

Whale Man quickly turned, dived into the water, and swam swiftly after the disappearing canoe. By the time he'd reached the other side, Koala Man and all the other creatures had long since disappeared. Before they left, they pushed the canoe off into the water and it floated away. It's still floating out there, somewhere, around the coast of Australia.

Whale Man never gave up hunting for his canoe. To this day, he swims around and around Australia, still searching the oceans for his stolen canoe.

You can see him swimming out there, spouting water through the hole in his head, made by the Starfish Man when they fought that day, way back in the Dreamtime.

Turtle, Oyster and Whale

Oyster was married to Sea Turtle.

For a time they lived happily together, but after a while Turtle grew tired of her husband's incessant demands. He was sitting huddled up on the beach with his head touching his knees, expecting her to do all the work.

'Hurry up, wife,' he called. 'I'm thirsty. I want you to dig a well in the sand.'

Turtle looked at him coldly.

'You have as many hands as I have,' she said in a shrill voice.

'Never mind how many hands I have,' Oyster retorted. 'Get to work with your own and dig that well for me.'

She stood over him and spread out her hands.

'Two hands for cutting firewood,' she said. 'Two hands for making a fire. Two hands for building the wurley. Two hands for cooking the morning meal. What hands will I use for digging a well? It's time you used your two hands to do some work.'

Oyster jumped up and hit her on the face and body.

'Two hands to hit you with,' he mocked her. 'How do you like that, little Turtle wife?'

Miintinta the Turtle woman didn't like it at all. She picked up her husband and dumped him on the sand so hard that he nearly broke in two. He caught her by the neck and dragged her down. They rolled over and over on the sand, hitting and kicking and making so much noise that Akama the Whale heard it. He was travelling up the coast and turned aside to see what was happening.

He looked down at them with a smile. He was a big man. Two enormous hands picked up Oyster and Turtle and held them apart.

'You are old enough to know better than to fight like wild animals,' he reproved them. 'There, see if you can behave yourselves now,' and he put them on their feet.

Never before had Whale been so surprised. Forgetting all about her husband, Turtle flew at him, biting and scratching, while Oyster picked up a digging stick and hit him on the back.

'What have I done?' Whale cried. 'I was only trying to help you.'

'Then get away as fast as you can and never interfere again between husband and wife.' Akama looked at them with a puzzled expression.

'All right!' he said hastily as Oyster took a step towards him, and he ran away as fast as his legs would carry him.

Whale never stops on his long trip up the coast now, for he has learned to mind his own business. Turtle is still busy with her hands, digging in the soft, warm sand and laying her eggs in the holes she makes.

Australian Aboriginal legend

Tinirau and His Pet Whale

Tinirau was a great chief, famous throughout the land for his handsome looks and his noble bearing. But he was even better known for his school of whales.

When he called them, they would come and play off shore, cruising round in circles and blowing spray through their vent holes. His favourite was Tutunui, the largest of his whales. Tinirau liked nothing better than to climb upon his back and ride him through the breakers, and out into the stormy sea. He would look down on the flying waves and feel safe, as if he were on an island …

Tinirau stood on the shore and began calling, 'Tutunui, Tutunui! Come at once. I need you.'

'Who are you calling?' said Kae, shading his eyes and looking out to sea. 'There is nobody out there.'

But Tinirau went on calling, until the sea heaved and swirled, as the huge bulk of Tutunui, streaming with water, rose into view. Tinirau went up to him and, to Kae's astonishment, cut off a large slice of his flesh.

'He is so big,' said Tinirau, 'he will never miss it.' He gave the flesh to the women, and they cooked it, and gave a piece to Kae, who swore that he had never eaten flesh that had tasted better.

But now it was time to go. Kae, who had an evil plan in his mind, went up to Tinirau and said, 'My home is far away, and my friends must miss me. Lend me your whale so that I can get home quickly.'

When Tinirau looked doubtful, Kae said, 'Who baptised your son? Was it not I? Lend me your whale. It is but a small favour that I ask of you.'

Tinirau was very reluctant to lend his whale, but he did not wish to offend Kae by refusing, for as well as being a priest, Kae was a magician who had the power to harm him, if he chose to.

'Very well,' he said, 'but you must be careful, especially as you approach land. The whale knows when it is not safe for him to go further. As soon as he gives a shake, you must get off. If you stay on his back, he will keep going until he becomes stranded in shallow water, where he will die.'

'I understand,' said Kae. 'I shall do nothing to endanger him.'

Then he climbed on to the back of the huge beast, and it seemed no time before he was approaching the shore of his village. There was his carved meeting-house looking handsome in the sunlight. There were his children running down to the shore. Shouting and pointing their fingers at the strange sight of their father on the back of a whale.

He felt the whale give a shake, but he took no notice. The children were close now, and were coming closer. The whale gave another shake, but now it was too late. He had gone too far and was well and truly stranded.

What a feast was held that night in Kae's village! The rich smell of cooked flesh rose from the ovens, and was carried by the wind far along the coast to where Tinirau was standing, waiting for his pet to return.

'Alas!' he said. 'That is the sweet smell of Tutunui that the north wind brings to me.' And he went to his house and wept, and his sisters gathered round and wept with him.

Maori legend

The Whale Rider

She had reached the whale and was hanging onto its jaw. 'Greetings, ancient one', Kahu said as she clung onto the whale's jaw. 'Greetings.' She patted the whale and looking into its eye, said, 'I have come to you'.

The swell lifted her up and propelled her away from the head of the whale. She choked with the water and tried to dog paddle back to the whale's eye.

'Help me', she cried. 'Ko Kahutia Te Rangi au. Ko Paikea.'

The whale shuddered at the words.

Ko Paikea?

Ko Kahutia Te Rangi?

By chance, Kahu felt the whale's forward fin. Her fingers tightened quickly around it. She held on for dear life.

And the whale felt a surge of gladness which, as it mounted, became ripples of ecstasy, ever increasing. He began to communicate his joy to all parts of his body.

Out beyond the breakwater the herd suddenly became alert. With hope rising, they began to sing their encouragement to their leader.

The elderly female whales skirled their happiness through the sea. They listened as the pulsing strength of their leader manifested itself in stronger and stronger whalesong. They crooned tenderness back to him and then throbbed a communication to the younger males to assist their leader. The males arranged themselves in arrow formation to spear through the raging surf.

In the sunless sea sixty whales were sounding slowly, steeply diving. An ancient bull whale, twenty metres long and bearing a sacred sign, was in the middle of the herd. Flanking him were seven females, half his size, like black-gowned women, shepherding him gently downward.

'Haramai, haramai e koro', the women sibilantly sang. 'Tomo mai i waenganui i o tatou iwi', Come old one. Join us, your whole tribe in the sea.

The sea hissed and sparkled with love for the ancient bull whale and, every now and then, the old mother whale would close in on him, gently, to nuzzle him, caress him, and kiss him just to let him know how much he had been missed. But in her heart of hearts she knew that he was badly wounded and near to exhaustion.

From the corner of her eye, the old mother whale noticed a small white shape clasping her husband just behind his tattooed head. She rose to observe the figure and then drifted back beside him.

'Ko wai te tekoteko kei runga?' she sang, her voice musically pulsing. 'Who are you carrying?'

'Ko Paikea, ko Paikea', the bull whale responded, and the bass notes boomed like an organ through the subterranean cathedral of the sea. 'I am carrying my lord, Paikea.'

The sea was a giant liquid sky and the whales were descending, plummeting downward like ancient dreams. On either side of the bull whale and his female entourage were warrior whales, ike hokowhitu a Tu, swift and sturdy, always alert, a phalanx of fierceness.

'Keep close ranks', the warrior whales warned. 'Neke neke.'

The leader signalled to some of the warriors to fall back to the rear to close up and tighten the remaining herd of women, men and children.

Meanwhile, the old mother whale was processing the information that the bull whale had given her. 'Ko Paikea? Ko Paikea?' The other women caught flashes of her puzzlement and, curious themselves, rose to look at the motionless rider. One of them nudged the tiny shape and saw a white face like a sleeping dolphin. The female whales hummed their considerations among themselves, trying to figure it all out. Then they shrugged. If the bull whale said it was Paikea, it was Paikea. After all, the bull whale was the boss, the chief.

'Keep close ranks', the warrior whales whistled reprovingly.

The whales shifted closer together, to support one another, as they fell through the sea.

Then one day, at its noon apex, the first sighting was made. A spume on the horizon. A dark shape rising from the greenstone depths of the ocean, awesome, leviathan, breaching through the surface and hurling itself skyward before falling seaward again. Underwater the muted thunder boomed like a great door opening far away, and both sea and land trembled from the impact of that downward plunging. Suddenly the sea was filled with awesome singing, a song with eternity in it, a song to the land: You have called and I have come, bearing the gift of the Gods. The dark shape rising, rising again. A whale, gigantic. A sea monster. Just as it burst through the sea, a flying fish leaping high in its ecstasy saw water and air streaming like thunderous foam from that noble beast and knew, ah yes, that the time had come. For the sacred sign was on the monster, a swirling tattoo imprinted on the forehead. Then the flying fish saw that astride the head, as it broke skyward, was a man. He was wondrous to look upon, the whale rider. The water streamed away from him and he opened his mouth to gasp in the cold air. His eyes were shining with splendor. His body dazzled with diamond spray. Upon that beast he looked like a small tattooed figurine, dark brown, glistening, and erect. He seemed, with all his strength, to be pulling the whale into the sky.

Witi Ihimaera, *The Whale Rider*, 1987

A dark shape rising from the greenstone depths of the ocean, awesome, leviathan, breaching through the surface and hurling itself skyward before falling seaward again.

Witi Ihimaera, *The Whale Rider*, 1987

The Whale Tooth

Another canoe journeyed up the Rewa that day. But it journeyed an hour astern, and it took care not to be seen. This canoe was also the property of Ra Vatu. In it was Erirola, Ra Vatu's first cousin and trusted henchman; and in the small basket that never left his hand was a whale tooth. It was a magnificent tooth, fully six inches long, beautifully proportioned, the ivory turned yellow and purple with age. This tooth was likewise the property of Ra Vatu; and in Fiji, when such a tooth goes forth, things usually happen. For this is the virtue of the whale tooth: Whoever accepts it cannot refuse the request that may accompany it or follow it. The request may be anything from a human life to a tribal alliance, and no Fijian is so dead to honor as to deny the request when once the tooth has been accepted. Sometimes the request hangs fire, or the fulfilment is delayed, with untoward consequences.

Jack London, 'The Whale Tooth', *South Sea Tales*, 1911

Anguta threw his daughter overboard into the icy sea, and when she clutched at the side of the boat, he chopped her fingers off. Some of the fingers sank into the sea and became whales, fish and other sea creatures.

Inuit myth

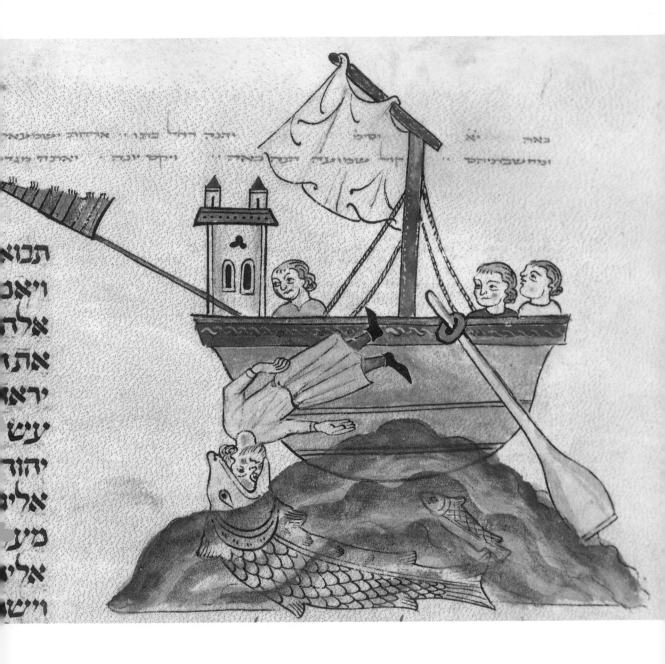

יהגד הזל בזאו ארחה ישבי ראא   באה   יא
וכה שבעיהם   קול פמו גה הזק האה   ויקק ינה   יאהד מגד

תכוא
וייא
אלה
אתי
ירא
יעש
יהוה
אלי
מע
אלי
ויש

Chewa the Giant Whale

This is the story of how Chewa the Whale, the king of fish, has an enormous mouth. One day Chewa's father died. Upon hearing the news Chewa patiently remarked 'It is God's work'. After a number of years his mother died. Again, upon hearing the news Chewa only said 'It is God's work'. However, after a few years Chewa's wife died. This time Chewa was grief-stricken and opened his mouth wide and mournfully uttered 'Ah, ah, ah!'. His grief-stricken state was so desperate and lasted so long that as he continued to cry out, his mouth grew wider and wider.

SWAHILI LEGEND

Big Raven and the Stranded Whale

Big Raven, was out walking one day and came upon a whale stranded on the beach. The desperate whale begged Big Raven to help him get back into the water. However, the whale was so enormous and Big Raven was not strong enough to pull the whale by himself. So he asked the Great Spirit for help. The Great Spirit told Big Raven to go and find the magic mushrooms in the forest which were growing in moonlight. If he ate these, he would have the necessary strength. Big Raven found the mushrooms and was able to rescue the whale.

INUIT LEGEND

THE *Ball Game*
BY THE SACO

Water-goblins from the streams about Katahdin had left their birthplace and journeyed away to the Agiochooks, making their presence known to the Indians of that region by thefts and loss of life. When the manitou, Glooskap, learned that these goblins were eating human flesh and committing other outrages, he took on their own form, turning half his body into stone, and went in search of them. The wigwam had been pitched near the Home of the Water Fairies — a name absurdly changed by the people of North Conway to Diana's Bath — and on entering he was invited to take meat. The tail of a whale was cooked and offered to him, but after he had taken it upon his knees one of the goblins exclaimed, 'That is too good for a beggar like you,' and snatched it away. Glooskap had merely to wish the return of the dainty when it flew back into his platter. Then he took the whale's jaw, and snapped it like a reed; he filled his pipe and burned the tobacco to ashes in one inhalation; when his hosts closed the wigwam and smoked vigorously, intending to foul the air and stupefy him, he enjoyed it, while they grew sick; so they whispered to each other, 'This is a mighty magician, and we must try his powers in another way.'

A game of ball was proposed, and, adjourning to a sandy level at the bend of the Saco, they began to play, but Glooskap found that the ball was a hideous skull that rolled and snapped at him and would have torn his flesh had it not been immortal and immovable from his bones. He crushed it at a blow, and breaking off the bough of a tree he turned it by a word into a skull ten times larger than the other that flew after the wicked people as a wildcat leaps upon a rabbit. Then the god stamped on the sands and all the springs were opened in the mountains, so that the Saco came rising through the valley with a roar that made the nations tremble. The goblins were caught in the flood and swept into the sea, where Glooskap changed them into fish.

Native American legend

SIMILARLY AMONG THE ALEUTS OF ALASKA
THE HUNTER WHO HAD STRUCK A WHALE
WITH A CHARMED SPEAR WOULD NOT THROW
AGAIN, BUT RETURNED AT ONCE TO HIS
HOME AND SEPARATED HIMSELF FROM HIS
PEOPLE IN A HUT SPECIALLY CONSTRUCTED
FOR THE PURPOSE, WHERE HE STAYED FOR THREE
DAYS WITHOUT FOOD OR DRINK AND WITHOUT
TOUCHING OR LOOKING UPON A WOMAN.

Sir James George Frazer, *The Golden Bough*, 1922

Chapter 3

THE *idea* OF MIRACLE

Imagining the whale

The whale has always been a bountiful source of inspiration for writers and poets, and even humorists. The large size of the whale has made it the subject of much metaphor, perhaps most notably in Thomas Hobbes's *Leviathan*, where 'Leviathan' (a sea monster or whale), is a symbol for the State, and in Herman Melville's *Moby Dick*, where the author opines that 'all men live enveloped in whale-lines'. Writers have ruminated on the unusual appearance of the whale — 'a gigantic tadpole' says Ambrose Bierce in his satirical *Devil's Dictionary*, and 'not a table fish' notes Hilaire Belloc. In fact, many of the world's greatest writers have paused for thought about the whale, including Virgil, Shakespeare, Swift, Milton, Blake, Dickens, Keats, Cooper and, of course, Melville. Whales, or whale-like creatures, also make an appearance in the world's most popular children's literature, too, namely Hans Christian Andersen's *The Little Mermaid* and Carlo Collodi's *Pinocchio*.

All men live enveloped in whale-lines. All are born with halters round their necks; but it is only when caught in the swift, sudden turn of death, that mortals realize the silent, subtle, ever present perils of life.

Herman Melville, *Moby Dick*, 1851

st belua inmari q̃ grece aspido delone dr̄. latine uͥ
aspido testudo. lete z dicta. ob immanitatem coꝛ

Arm'd with Ribs of Whale

To Fifty chosen Sylphs, of special Note, We trust th' important Charge, the Petticoat. Oft have we known that sev'nfold Fence to fail; Tho' stiff with Hoops, and arm'd with Ribs of Whale.

Alexander Pope, *Rape of the Lock*, 1712

Gulliver in Brobdingnag

... now and then they take a whale that happens to be dashed against the rocks, which the common people feed on heartily. These whales I have known so large, that a man could hardly carry one upon his shoulders; and sometimes, for curiosity, they are brought in hampers to Lorbrulgrud; I saw one of them in a dish at the king's table, which passed for a rarity, but I did not observe he was fond of it; for I think, indeed, the bigness disgusted him, although I have seen one somewhat larger in Greenland.

Jonathan Swift, *Gulliver's Travels*, 1726

The Whale

THE WHALE THAT WANDERS ROUND THE POLE

IS NOT A TABLE FISH.

YOU CANNOT BAKE OR BOIL HIM WHOLE

NOR SERVE HIM IN A DISH;

BUT YOU MAY CUT HIS BLUBBER UP

AND MELT IT DOWN FOR OIL.

AND SO REPLACE THE COLZA BEAN

(A PRODUCT OF THE SOIL).

THESE FACTS SHOULD ALL BE NOTED DOWN

AND RUMINATED ON,

BY EVERY BOY IN OXFORD TOWN

WHO WANTS TO BE A DON.

Hilaire Belloc, *The Bad Child's Book of Beasts*, 1896

Oil? What do you take me for? I'm not a whaler.

Mark Twain, *Roughing It*, 1872

How the Whale Got His Throat

In the sea, once upon a time, O my Best Beloved, there was a Whale, and he ate fishes … All the fishes he could find in all the sea he ate with his mouth — so! Till at last there was only one small fish left in all the sea, and he was a small 'Stute Fish, and he swam a little behind the Whale's right ear, so as to be out of harm's way. Then the Whale stood up on his tail and said, 'I'm hungry'. And the small 'Stute Fish said in a small 'stute voice, 'Noble and generous Cetacean, have you ever tasted Man?'.

'No,' said the Whale. 'What is it like?'

'Nice,' said the small 'Stute Fish. 'Nice but nubbly.'

'Then fetch me some,' said the Whale, and he made the sea froth up with his tail.

'One at a time is enough,' said the 'Stute Fish. 'If you swim to latitude Fifty North, longitude Forty West (that is magic), you will find, sitting on a raft, in the middle of the sea, with nothing on but a pair of blue canvas breeches, a pair of suspenders (you must not forget the suspenders, Best Beloved), and a jack-knife, one ship-wrecked Mariner, who, it is only fair to tell you, is a man of infinite-resource-and-sagacity.'

So the Whale swam and swam to latitude Fifty North, longitude Forty West, as fast as he could swim, and on a raft, in the middle of the sea, with nothing to wear except a pair of blue canvas breeches, a pair of suspenders (you must particularly remember the suspenders, Best Beloved), and a jack-knife, he found one single, solitary shipwrecked Mariner, trailing his toes in the water. (He had his mummy's leave to paddle, or else he would never have done it, because he was a man of infinite-resource-and-sagacity.)

Then the Whale opened his mouth back and back and back till it nearly touched his tail, and he swallowed the shipwrecked Mariner, and the raft he was sitting on, and his blue canvas breeches, and the suspenders (which you must not forget), and the jack-knife — He swallowed them all down into his warm, dark, inside cup-boards, and then he smacked his lips — so, and turned round three times on his tail.

But as soon as the Mariner, who was a man of infinite-resource-and-sagacity, found himself truly inside the Whale's warm, dark, inside cup-boards, he stumped and he jumped and he thumped and he bumped, and he pranced and he danced, and he banged and he clanged, and he hit and he bit, and he leaped and he creeped, and he prowled and he howled, and he hopped and he dropped, and he cried and he sighed, and he crawled and he bawled, and he stepped and he lepped, and he danced hornpipes where he shouldn't, and the Whale felt most unhappy indeed. (Have you forgotten the suspenders?)

So he said to the 'Stute Fish, 'This man is very nubbly, and besides he is making me hiccough. What shall I do?'

'Tell him to come out,' said the 'Stute Fish.

So the Whale called down his own throat to the shipwrecked Mariner, 'Come out and behave yourself. I've got the hiccoughs.'

'Nay, nay!' said the Mariner. 'Not so, but far otherwise. Take me to my natal-shore and the white-cliffs-of-Albion, and I'll think about it.' And he began to dance more than ever.

'You had better take him home,' said the 'Stute Fish to the Whale. 'I ought to have warned you that he is a man of infinite-resource-and-sagacity.'

So the Whale swam and swam and swam, with both flippers and his tail, as hard as he could for the hiccoughs; and at last he saw the Mariner's natal-shore and the white-cliffs-of-Albion, and he rushed half-way up the beach, and opened his mouth wide and wide and wide, and said, 'Change here for Winchester, Ashuelot, Nashua, Keene, and stations on the Fitchburg Road'; and just as he said 'Fitch' the Mariner walked out of his mouth. But while the Whale had been swimming, the Mariner, who was indeed a person of infinite-resource-and-sagacity, had taken his jack-knife and cut up the raft into a little square grating all running criss-cross, and he had tied it firm with his suspenders (now, you know why you were not to forget the suspenders!), and he dragged that grating good and tight into the Whale's throat, and there it stuck! ...

For the Mariner he was also an Hi-ber-ni-an. And he stepped out on the shingle, and went home to his mother, who had given him leave to trail his toes in the water; and he married and lived happily ever afterward. So did the Whale. But from that day on, the grating in his throat, which he could neither cough up nor swallow down, prevented him eating anything except very, very small fish; and that is the reason why whales nowadays never eat men or boys or little girls ...

WHEN the cabin port-holes are dark and green
Because of the seas outside;
When the ship goes wop (with a wiggle between)
And the steward falls into the soup-tureen,
And the trunks begin to slide;
When Nursey lies on the floor in a heap,
And Mummy tells you to let her sleep,
And you aren't waked or washed or dressed,
Why, then you will know (if you haven't guessed)
You're 'Fifty North and Forty West!'

Rudyard Kipling, *Just So Stories*, 1902

A RATHER *Large Whale*

While we were all in a state of astonishment at the general and unaccountable confusion in which we were involved, the whole was suddenly explained by the appearance of a large whale, which had been basking, asleep, within sixteen feet of the surface of the water. This animal was so much displeased with the disturbance which our ship had given him — for in our passage we had with our rudder scratched his nose — that he beat in all the gallery and part of the quarter-deck with his tail, and almost at the same instant took the main-sheet anchor, which was suspended, as it usually is, from the head, between his teeth, and ran away with the ship at least sixty leagues, at the rate of twelve leagues an hour, when, fortunately, the cable broke, and we lost both the whale and the anchor. However, upon our return to Europe, some months after, we found the same whale within a few leagues of the same spot, floating dead upon the water. It measured above half a mile in length. As we could take only a small quantity of such a monstrous animal on board, we got our boats out, and with much difficulty cut off his head, where, to our great joy, we found the anchor, and above forty fathoms of the cable, concealed on the left side of his mouth, just under his tongue. Perhaps this was the cause of his death, as that side of his tongue was much swelled with severe inflammation.

Rudolph Erich Raspe, *The Surprising Adventures of Baron Münchausen*, 1785

A whale has no home. No Waldorf or Plaza or comfortable country house for his. He just floats around like a Gypsy.

Frank Finney, *A Woman Has an Awful Lot to Thank a Whale for*, 1909

Gigantic Tadpole

❧

LEVIATHAN, n. AN ENORMOUS AQUATIC ANIMAL
MENTIONED BY JOB. SOME SUPPOSE IT TO HAVE BEEN THE
WHALE, BUT THAT DISTINGUISHED ICHTHYOLOGER, DR.
JORDAN, OF STANFORD UNIVERSITY, MAINTAINS WITH
CONSIDERABLE HEAT THAT IT WAS A SPECIES OF GIGANTIC
TADPOLE (THADDEUS POLANDENSIS) OR POLLIWIG — MARIA
PSEUDO-HIRSUTA. FOR AN EXHAUSTIVE DESCRIPTION AND
HISTORY OF THE TADPOLE CONSULT THE FAMOUS MONOGRAPH
OF JANE POTTER, THADDEUS OF WARSAW.

❧

Ambrose Bierce,
The Devil's Dictionary, 1911

The Chanting of the Whales

North to the Pole, south to the Pole
The whales of California wallow and roll.
They dive and breed and snort and play
And the sun struck feed them every day
Boatloads of citrons, quinces, cherries,
Of bloody strawberries, plums and beets,
Hogsheads of pomegranates, vats of sweets,
And the he-whales' chant like a cyclone blares,
Proclaiming the California noons
So gloriously hot some days
The snake is fried in the desert
And the flea no longer plays.
There are ten gold suns in California
When all other lands have one,
For the Golden Gate must have due light
And persimmons be well-done.
And the hot whales slosh and cool in the wash
And the fume of the hollow sea.
Rally and roam in the loblolly foam
And whoop that their souls are free.

Lindsay Vachel, 'The Golden Whales of California', 1920

Her lips curved downwards instantly, As if
of india-rubber. 'Hounds IN FULL CRY
I like,' said she: (Oh how I longed to snub
her!) 'Of fish, a whale's the one for me,
IT IS SO FULL OF BLUBBER!'

Lewis Carroll, 'Melancholetta', 1869

Hitchhiker's GUIDE TO WHALES

Douglas Adams, *The Hitchhiker's Guide to the Galaxy*, 1979

Another thing that got forgotten was the fact that against all probability a sperm whale had suddenly been called into existence several miles above the surface of an alien planet.

And since this is not a naturally tenable position for a whale, this poor innocent creature had very little time to come to terms with its identity as a whale before it then had to come to terms with not being a whale any more.

This is a complete record of its thought from the moment it began its life till the moment it ended it.

Ah …! What's happening? It thought.

Er, excuse me, who am I?

Hello?

Why am I here? What's my purpose in life?

What do I mean by who am I?

Calm down, get a grip now … Oh! This is an interesting sensation, what is it? It's a sort of … yawning, tingling sensation in my … my … well, I suppose I'd better start finding names for things if I want to make any headway in what for the sake of what I shall call an argument I shall call the world, so let's call it my stomach.

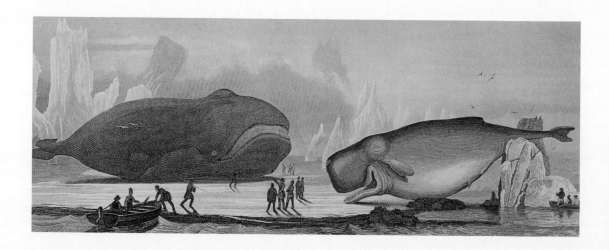

Good. Ooooh, it's getting quite strong. And hey, what about this whistling roaring sound going past what I'm suddenly going to call my head? Perhaps I can call that ... wind! Is that a good name? It'll do ... perhaps I can find a better name for it later when I've found out what it's for. It must be something very important because there certainly seems to be a hell of a lot of it. Hey! What's this thing? This ... let's call it a tail — yeah, tail. Hey! I can really thrash it about pretty good, can't I? Wow! Wow! That feels great! Doesn't seem to achieve very much but I'll probably find out what it's for later on. Now — have I built up any coherent picture of things yet?

No.

Never mind, hey, this is really exciting, so much to find out about, so much to look forward to, I'm quite dizzy with anticipation ...

Or is it the wind?

There really is a lot of that now, isn't there?

And wow! Hey! What's this thing suddenly coming towards me very fast? Very very fast. So big and flat and round, it needs a big wide sounding name like ... ow ... ound ... round ... ground! That's it! That's a good name — ground!

I wonder if it will be friends with me?

And the rest, after a sudden wet thud, was silence.

Oh are you from Wales? Do you know
a fella named Jonah? He used to live in
whales for a while.

Groucho Marx

There is no eel so small but it hopes to become a whale.
Germanic proverb

ANALOGOUS TO THE WHALES

For by the ministry of thy holy ones, thy mysteries have made their way
amid the buffeting billows of the world to instruct the nations in thy name,
in thy Baptism. And among these things many great and marvelous works
have been wrought which are analogous to the huge whales.

St Augustine, *Confessions*, AD 397–98

Like as the Wounded Whale

*Which to secure, no skill of leach's art Mote him availle, but to returne againe To
his wound's worker, that with lowly dart, Dinting his breast, had bred his restless
paine, Like as the wounded whale to shore flies thro' the maine.*

Edmund Spenser, *The Faerie Queene*, 1590

Jonas and the Whale

Verily Jonas too is among the envoys;
When he ran away to the loaded ship;
He cast lots, but was one of those who drew blank.
So the whale swallowed him, he being to blame.
And had it not been that he was one of those who give glory,
He would have remained in its belly until the day of their being raised up.

The Qur'an, Sura 37

DESPOISSONS

J.P. Aubry. fec.

THE
Progress
of the SOUL

❧

HE HUNTS NOT FISH, BUT AS AN OFFICER,

STAYES IN HIS COURT, AT HIS OWNE NET, AND THERE

ALL SUITORS OF ALL SORTS THEMSELVES ENTHRALL;

SO ON HIS BACKE LYES THIS WHALE WANTONING,

AND IN HIS GULFE-LIKE THROAT, SUCKS EVERY THING

THAT PASSETH NEARE. FISH CHASETH FISH, AND ALL,

FLYER AND FOLLOWER, IN THIS WHIRLEPOOLE FALL;

O MIGHT NOT STATES OF MORE EQUALITY

CONSIST? AND IS IT OF NECESSITY

THAT THOUSAND GUILTLESSE SMALS,

TO MAKE ONE GREAT, MUST DIE?

❧

John Donne, *The Progress of the Soul*, 1601

The Whale and the Fry

First Fish. Why, as men do a-land; the great ones eat up the little ones; I can compare our rich misers to nothing so fitly as to a whale; a' plays and tumbles, driving the poor fry before him, and at last devours them all at a mouthful. Such whales have I heard on o' the land, who never leave gaping till they've swallowed the whole parish, church, steeple, bells, and all.

Shakespeare, *Pericles Prince of Tyre*, Act II, Scene I, c.1604

'LEVIATHAN'

NATURE, the art whereby God hath made and governs the world, is by the art of man so imitated that he can make an artificial animal. For by art is created that great leviathan called a commonwealth or state, which is but an artificial man; in which the sovereignty is an artificial soul, as giving life and motion; the magistrates and other officers the joints; reward and punishment the nerves; concord, health; discord, sickness; lastly, the pacts or covenants by which the parts were first set together resemble the fiat' of God at the Creation.

Thomas Hobbes, *Leviathan*, 1651

He knows where the whales breed.
(Said of one who pretends to knowledge of everything.)

Gaelic proverb

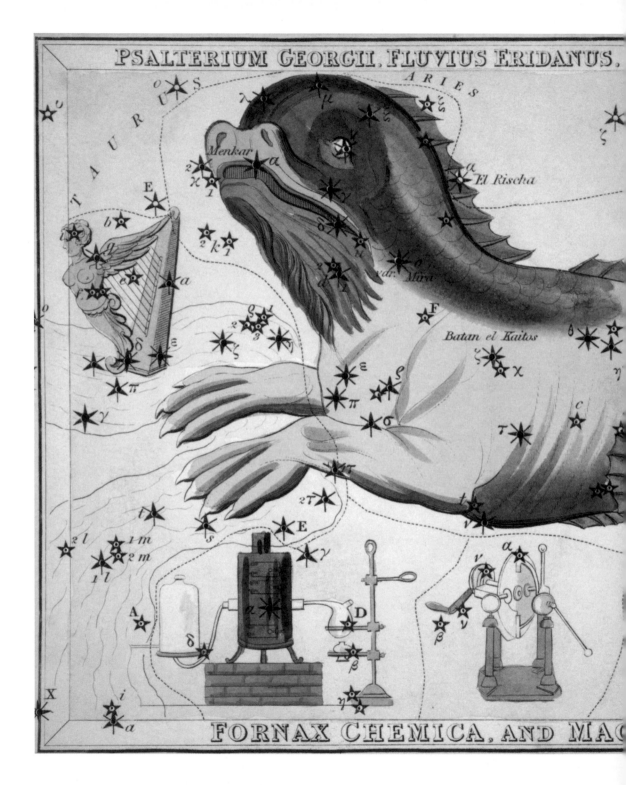

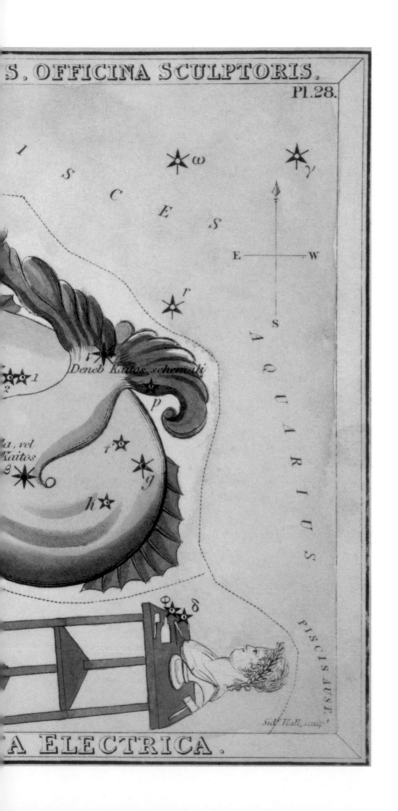

ω

γ

N

E W

S

r

s

Deneb Kaitos schemali

i

1

2

p

a, vel
Kaitos

t a

g

h

φ

δ

A ELECTRICA.

PISCIS AUST.

Sid.ᵗ Hall, sculp.ᵗ

P I S C E S

A Q U A R I U S

THE EYE OF ENVIE

YET SOMETIMES WITH THE EYE OF ENVIE, WHICH ENLARGES
OBJECTS LIKE A MULTIPLYING GLASS, THEY BEHOLD THESE
STATESMEN, AND THINK THEM IMMENSE AS WHALES, THE
MOTION OF WHOSE VAST BODIES CAN IN A PEACEFULL CALM
TROUBLE THE OCEAN TILL IT BOYL.

⤳

Sir William D'Avenant,
Preface to Gondibert, an Heroik Poem, 1651

When Seamen
MEET A WHALE

The wits of the present age being so very numerous and penetrating, it seems the grandees of Church and State begin to fall under horrible apprehensions lest these gentlemen, during the intervals of a long peace, should find leisure to pick holes in the weak sides of religion and government. To prevent which, there has been much thought employed of late upon certain projects for taking off the force and edge of those formidable inquirers from canvassing and reasoning upon such delicate points. They have at length fixed upon one, which will require some time as well as cost to perfect. Meanwhile, the danger hourly increasing, by new levies of wits, all appointed (as there is reason to fear) with pen, ink, and paper, which may at an hour's warning be drawn out into pamphlets and other offensive weapons ready for immediate execution, it was judged of absolute necessity that some present expedient be thought on till the main design can be brought to maturity. To this end, at a grand committee, some days ago, this important discovery was made by a certain curious and refined observer, that seamen have a custom when they meet a Whale to fling him out an empty Tub, by way of amusement, to divert him from laying violent hands upon the Ship. This parable was immediately mythologised; the Whale was interpreted to be Hobbes's 'Leviathan', which tosses and plays with all other schemes of religion and government, whereof a great many are hollow, and dry, and empty, and noisy, and wooden, and given to rotation. This is the Leviathan from whence the terrible wits of our age are said to borrow their weapons. The Ship in danger is easily understood to be its old antitype the commonwealth. But how to analyse the Tub was a matter of difficulty, when, after long inquiry and debate, the literal meaning was preserved, and it was decreed that, in order to prevent these Leviathans from tossing and sporting with the commonwealth, which of itself is too apt to fluctuate, they should be diverted from that game by 'A Tale of a Tub.' And my genius being conceived to lie not unhappily that way, I had the honour done me to be engaged in the performance.

Jonathan Swift, *A Tale of a Tub*, 1704

Nearer to the Idea of Miracle

The story of the whale swallowing Jonah, though a whale is large enough to do it, borders greatly on the marvelous; but it would have approached nearer to the idea of miracle if Jonah had swallowed the whale.

Thomas Paine, *The Age of Reason*, 1794

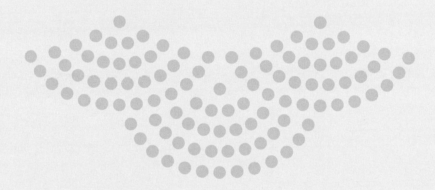

Drinking My Soul Away

I see a serpent in Canada who courts me to his love,
In Mexico an Eagle, and a Lion in Peru;
I see a Whale in the South-sea, drinking my soul away.

William Blake, 'America: A Prophecy', 1793

The Prince of Wales

Io! Paean! Io! sing.
To the finny people's king.
Not a mightier whale than this
In the vast Atlantic is;
Not a fatter fish than he,
Flounders round the Polar Sea.

Charles Lamb, *The Triumph of the Whale*, 1812

'THE PRINCE OF WHALES OR THE FISHERMAN AT ANCHOR.

All That Most Maddens and Torments

All that most maddens and torments; all that stirs up the lees of things; all truth with malice in it; all that cracks the sinews and cakes the brain; all the subtle demonisms of life and thought; all evil, to crazy Ahab, were visibly personified, and made practically assailable in Moby Dick. He piled upon the whale's white hump the sum of all the general rage and hate felt by his whole race from Adam down; and then, as if his chest had been a mortar, he burst his hot heart's shell upon it.

Herman Melville, *Moby Dick*, 1851

ETHER 2:3, The Book of Mormon

For behold, ye shall be as a whale in the midst of the sea; for the mountain waves shall dash upon you.

WHALE: to throw dice or to be very active in some other gambling activity; to do anything very effectively.

Clarence Major, *Black Slang: A Dictionary of Afro-American Talk*, 1978

Girls and Whales

Girls are so different from whales — at least to whalemen. For you get fast to a whale and if he runs, you run; or if he goes down, you wait till he comes up again … But with girls it's more complicated. Sometimes you're not fast to them when you think you are. Sometimes they go down and never come up again. And when you're a whaleman you've little time for courting. The stay in a home port is shockingly short.

Captain Charles Robbins, *The Gam: Being a Group of Whaling Stories*, 1899

Very like a whale

Very much like a cock-and-bull story; a fudge. Hamlet chaffs Polo'nius by comparing a cloud to a camel, and then to a weasel, and when the courtier assents Hamlet adds, 'Or like a whale'; to which Polonius answers, 'Very like a whale'. (Act iii. 2.)

Brewer's Dictionary of Phrase and Fable, 1898

LONESOMENESS LIKE A WHALE

Just now have I seen them bent down — to creep to the cross. Around light and liberty did they once flutter like gnats and young poets. A little older, a little colder: and already are they mystifiers, and mumblers and mollycoddlers. Did perhaps their hearts despond, because lonesomeness had swallowed me like a whale? Did their ear perhaps hearken yearningly — long for me in vain, and for my trumpet-notes and herald-calls?

Friedrich Nietzsche, *Thus Spake Zarathustra*, 1883–85

They halted, looking towards the blunt cape
of Bray Head that lay on the water like the snout of
a sleeping whale. Stephen freed his arm quietly.

James Joyce, *Ulysses*, 1922

Spain – a great whale stranded on the shores of Europe.
Edmund Burke (1729–1797)

If you were to make little fishes talk,
they would talk like whales.

Oliver Goldsmith (to Dr Johnson), in James Boswell, *Life of Johnson*, 1791

Spermaceti

I sound my sight, and flexing skeletons eddy
in our common wall. With a sonic bolt from the fragrant
chamber of my head, I burst the lives of some
and slow, backwashing them into my mouth. I lighten,
breathe, and laze below again. And peer in long low tones
over the curve of Hard to river-tasting and oil-tasting
coasts, to the grand grinding coasts of rigid air.
How the wall of our medium has a shining, pumping rim:
the withstood crush of deep flight in it, perpetual entry!
Only the holes of eyesight and breath still tie us
to the dwarf-making Air, where true sight barely functions.
The power of our wall likewise guards us from
slowness of the rock Hard, its life-powdering compaction,
from its fissures and streamy layers that we sing into sight
but are silent, fixed, disjointed in. Eyesight is a leakage
of nearby into us, and shows us the taste of food
conformed over its spines. But our greater sight is uttered.
I sing beyond the curve of distance the living joined bones
of my song-fellows; I sound a deep volcano's valve tubes
storming whitely in black weight; I receive an island's slump,
song-scrambling ship's heartbeats, and the sheer shear of current-forms
bracketing a seamount. The wall, which running blind I demolish,
heals, prickling me with sonars. My every long shaped cry
re-establishes the world, and centres its ringing structure.

Les Murray, 'Spermaceti', 1992

THE idea OF MIRACLE THE WHALES COMPANION

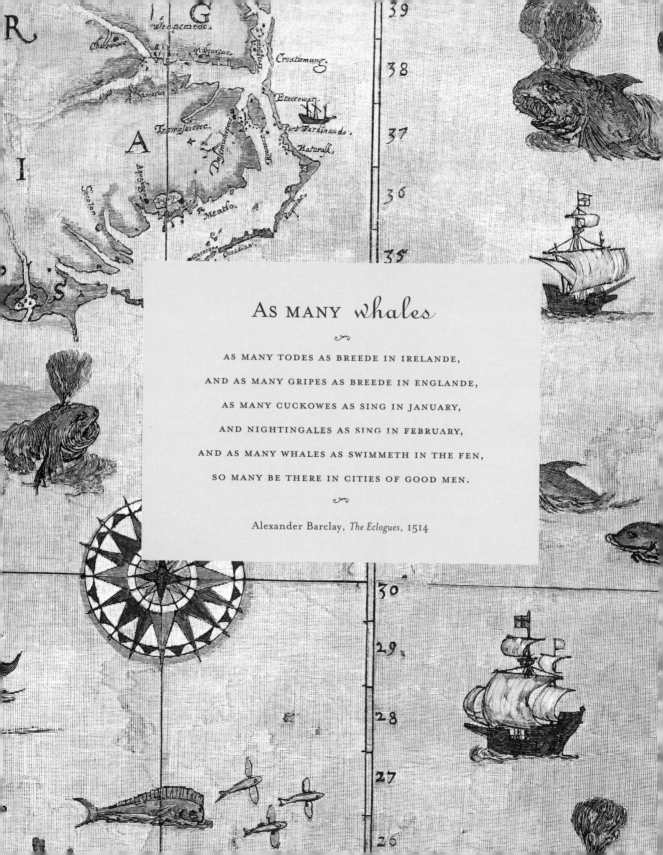

AS MANY whales

AS MANY TODES AS BREEDE IN IRELANDE,

AND AS MANY GRIPES AS BREEDE IN ENGLANDE,

AS MANY CUCKOWES AS SING IN JANUARY,

AND NIGHTINGALES AS SING IN FEBRUARY,

AND AS MANY WHALES AS SWIMMETH IN THE FEN,

SO MANY BE THERE IN CITIES OF GOOD MEN.

Alexander Barclay, *The Eclogues*, 1514

MONSTER WHALES

The tempests fly before their father's face,
Trains of inferior gods his triumph grace,
And monster whales before their master play,
And choirs of Tritons crowd the wat'ry way.

Virgil, *The Aeneid*, 1st century BC

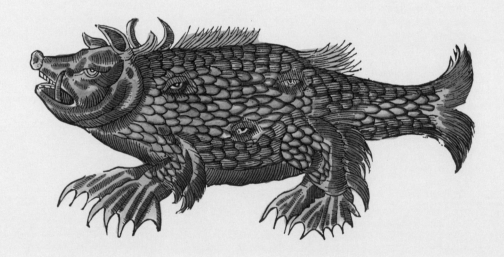

And that region which ... with its
wild race of fishermen for whom
no more than for their whales had
there been any Middle Ages.

Marcel Proust, *Swann's Way*, 1913

ON THE NATURE OF FISHES

Prodigious Fishes, of enormous Size,
With shiv'ring Fright pale Mariners surprize.
Nature's strange Work, vast Whales of diff'ring Form
Toss up the troubled Floods, and are themselves a Storm.
Uncouth the Sight, when They in dreadful Play
Discharge their Nostrils, and refund a Sea;
Or angry lash the Foam with hideous Sound,
And scatter all the wat'ry Dust around.
Fearless the fierce destructive Monsters roll,
Ingulph the Fish, and drive the flying Shoal.
In deepest Seas these living Isles appear,
And deepest Seas can Scarce the Pressure bear.
Their Bulk would more than fill the shelvy Straight,
And fathom'd Depths would yield beneath the Weight.

Such monstrous Kinds the fruitful Seas produce,
Yet such th' unconquer'd Force of Man subdues.
I sing the Toils, when stranded Whales invite
Couragious Fishers to the dreadful Fight.
While grander Scenes superior Ardour raise,
And nobler Argument exalts the Lays,
Great Substitutes of Jove, attend the Strain,
Ye Heav'n-built Walls, that guard his lower Reign.
Far in the middle Concave of the Deep
Their Residence the Whaly Monsters keep;
There rolling with unwieldy Pastime play,
Nor often from th' unfathom'd Bottom stray.
Eternal Appetite their Bowels gnaws,
And Famine fits enthron'd within their Jaws.
No Meats compose their glutted Teeth to rest,

Or fill th' unmeasur'd Chaos of their Breast.
On their own Kinds th' unnatural Gluttons feed,
And still the weaker by the stronger bleed.
The shudd'ring Sailor sees with wild Surprize
Their Backs above the breaking Surges rise,
Who Westward from Iberian Havens sails,
And fears a Shipwreck from their sporting Tails.
Erroneous from th' Atlantic Deep they glide,
And drive from either Fin a murm'ring Tide.
Not thus beneath a stately Galley's Oars
In frothy Curls the boiling Ocean roars.
When shallow Shores engage the flouncing Fiend,
Let all the Fishers wat'ry War descend.
All but the nimble Dog in sandy Chains
The shelving Margin of the Deep detains.
Their glimm'ring Eyes transmit a feeble Ray,
And vast unwieldy Limbs retard their Way.
But happy Friendship's faithful Aid supplies,
What partial Nature to their Sense denies.
A slender Fish conducts the Whaly Kind,
Slender his Size, but ample is his Mind:
Bold in the Front the little Pilot glides,
Averts their Dangers, and their Motions guides.
With grateful Joy the willing Whales attend,
Observe the Leader, and revere the Friend.
All to their little Chief obsequious roll:
Friendship has charms to sooth a savage Soul.
Between the distant Eyeballs of the Whale,
Th' impending Pilot waves his faithful Tail,
With Signs expressive points the doubtful Way,
And warns to fly the Shore, or chace the Prey.
The Tail as vocal with impulsive Air,
Bids him of all, but most of Man beware.

Oppian, *Halleuticks*, c.225

The Whale

THE EXETER BOOK, 10TH CENTURY

Now I will next, making use of my memory,
tell in verse, in the art of poetry,
about a kind of fish, about the great whale.
He is often met with, against their will,
by seafarers, and is dangerous and cruel
to every man. The name Fastitocalon
is given to this floater on the ancient seas.
His form is like a rough stone, as if
the largest of reed-beds, surrounded by sand-dunes,
were floating about by the shore of the sea,
so that voyagers think
that they are gazing at an island with their eyes;
and so they moor their high-prowed ships
by anchor-ropes to the supposed land,
stall their sea-horses at the edge of the water;
and then the stout-hearted men disembark
upon that island. Their ships remain
secure by the shore, surrounded by the tide.
Then the weary seafarers
encamp, and expect no danger.
They kindle a fire on that island,
set alight a high flame. The men are joyful;
tired out, they are glad of rest.
When, skilled in treachery, he feels
that the voyagers are securely settled upon him,
are encamped, enjoying the fine weather,
then suddenly the ocean creature
recklessly departs down
into the salt sea, makes for the bottom,
and, by drowning them, imprisons both ships
and men in the hall of death.

❧

The bold traveller through the sea
has another yet stranger characteristic.

When hunger oppresses him in the ocean
and the monster desires food,
then that warden of the sea opens his mouth,
his wide lips. A pleasant smell
comes from within him, so that other kinds of fish
are entrapped by means of it.
They swim with all speed to where the sweet smell
issues forth. They enter there
in an unwary crowd, until the wide mouth
is filled; then suddenly
he clashes together his grim jaws
around his plunder.

So it is with any man
who very often during this fleeting time
takes but careless regard of his life,
who lets vain desire delude him

by its sweet smell, so that he is, owing to his vices,
hateful to the King of glory. The accursed one
opens hell to him after his journey hence
and to those who frivolously and ill-advisedly,
against the guidance of the soul, fulfilled the joys
of the body.
When the deceiver, practised in evil,
has brought into that prison
where the fie is renewed, those who, loaded with sins,
adhered to him, and who once listened
eagerly to his teachings in the days of their life,
he then, after their death, clashes
fast together those grim jaws
the gates of hell. Those who enter there
have no return or escape, no egress ever,
any more than those fishes, swimmers in the sea,
may return from the grasp of the whale.

THOUGH IN A WHALE'S BELLY

'The mischief", said Don Quixote, 'was in my going off, for I should not have done so until I had seen thee paid; I should have known, from long experience, that no villain will keep his word if he finds it suits him to break it. But thou mayest remember, Andres, that I swore if he paid thee not I would track him down even though he were hidden in a whale's belly.'

Miguel Cervantes, *Don Quixote*, 1605

PARADISE LOST

Wallowing unwieldy, enormous in their gait
Tempest the ocean: there leviathan
Hugest of living creatures, on the deep
Stretched like a promontory sleeps or swims,
And seems a moving land, and at his gills
Draws in, and at his trunk spouts out a sea.

John Milton, *Paradise Lost*, Book VIII, 1667

THE SEAFARER

In the soul's secret chamber
My mind now is set,
My heart's thought, on wide waters,
The home of the whale;
It wanders away
Beyond limits of land:
Comes again to me, yearning
With eager desire;
Loud cries the lone-flier,
And stirs the mind's longing
To travel the way that is trackless,
The death-way over the flood.

Old English poem from *The Exeter Book*, 10th century

Pubd. March 14th 1806 by H Humphry 27 St. James's Street

POWDER

Js. Gillray invt. & ft.

__ a *TUB for the Whale!* { repr...

n Empty-Barrel tossed out to amuse the great LEVIATHAN-JOHN-BULL, in order
im from instantly laying violent hands upon ᵞ new Coalition Packet ─ Vide. Swift's Preface to the Tale of a Tub.

THROUGH GAPING JAWS

So close behind some promontory lie
The huge leviathans t' attend their prey;
And give no chase, but swallow in the fry,
Which through their gaping jaws mistake the way.

John Dryden, *Annus Mirabilis*, 1667

The Voyage

Woe to the sailor in this moment fell,
If yon light oar sweeps not his skiff afar
From that terrific storm which plagues the swell!
All speed away, all fly; the dying whale
Plunges, returns, and floats, so vast in scale
That still the winds and waves it seeming braves,
The while its cooling blood the billow laves.

Joseph Alphonse Esménard, 'The Voyage', 18th century

With gills pulmonic breathes the enormous Whale,
And spouts aquatic columns to the gale;
Sports on the shining wave at noontide hours,
And shifting rainbows crest the rising showers.

Erasmus Darwin, *The Temple of Nature*, Canto I, 1803

NEW YORK.—FIERCE FIGHT WITH AND CAPTURE OF TWO LARGE WHALES OFF AMAGANSETT, L. I., ON DECEMBER 12TH.
THE MONSTERS DIVING AFTER BEING HARPOONED.

FROM A SKETCH BY E. P. HUNTTING.—SEE PAGE 311.

ENDYMION

THE GULFING WHALE WAS LIKE A DOT IN THE SPELL,

YET LOOK UPON IT, AND 'T WOULD SIZE AND SWELL

TO ITS HUGE SELF; AND THE MINUTEST FISH

WOULD PASS THE VERY HARDEST GAZER'S WISH,

AND SHOW HIS LITTLE EYE'S ANATOMY.

John Keats, *Endymion*, 1817

The Little Mermaid

The dolphins were fun; they had turned somersaults, and the
big whales had spouted water up out of their nostrils; it was as
though there had been a hundred fountains all around.

Hans Christian Andersen, *The Little Mermaid*, 1837

He delivered Daniel from de lion's den,
Jonah from de belly of de whale.
And de Hebrew children from de fiery furnace,
An' why not everyman?

Didn't My Lord Deliver Daniel?, African American spiritual

WHALES AT SAN PEDRO

This being the spring season, San Pedro, as well as all the ports upon the coast, was filled
with whales, that had come in to make their annual visit upon soundings. For the first few
days that we were here and at Santa Barbara, we watched them with great interest — calling
out 'there she blows!' every time we saw the spout of one breaking the surface of the water;
but they soon became so common that we took little notice of them. They often 'broke' very
near us; and one thick, foggy night, during a dead calm, while I was standing anchor-watch,
one of them rose so near, that he struck our cable, and made all surge again. He did not
seem to like the encounter much himself, for he sheered off, and spouted at a good distance.

Richard Henry Dana, *Two Years Before the Mast*, 1840

On a Cruise for the Whale

We sail from Ravavai, an isle in the sea, not very far northward from the tropic of Capricorn, nor very far westward from Pitcairn's island, where the mutineers of the *Bounty* settled. At Ravavai I had stepped ashore some few months previous; and now was embarked on a cruise for the whale, whose brain enlightens the world.

And from Ravavai we sail for the Gallipagos, otherwise called the Enchanted Islands, by reason of the many wild currents and eddies there met.

Now, round about those isles, which Dampier once trod, where the Spanish bucaniers once hived their gold moidores, the Cachalot, or sperm whale, at certain seasons abounds …

In good time making the desired longitude upon the equator, a few leagues west of the Gallipagos, we spent several weeks chassezing across the Line, to and fro, in unavailing search for our prey. For some of their hunters believe, that whales, like the silver ore in Peru, run in veins through the ocean. So, day after day, daily; and week after week, weekly, we traversed the self-same longitudinal intersection of the self-same Line; till we were almost ready to swear that we felt the ship strike every time her keel crossed that imaginary locality …

But, at last after some time sailing due westward we quitted the Line in high disgust; having seen there, no sign of a whale.

But whither now? To the broiling coast of Papua? That region of sun-strokes, typhoons, and bitter pulls after whales unattainable. Far worse. We were going, it seemed, to illustrate the Whistonian theory concerning the damned and the comets; — hurried from equinoctial heats to arctic frosts. To be short, with the true fickleness of his tribe, our skipper had abandoned all thought of the Cachalot. In desperation, he was bent upon bobbing for the Right whale on the Nor' West Coast and in the Bay of Kamschatska.

To the uninitiated in the business of whaling, my feelings at this juncture may perhaps be hard to understand. But this much let me say: that Right whaling on the Nor' West Coast, in chill and dismal fogs, the sullen inert monsters rafting the sea all round like Hartz forest logs on the Rhine, and submitting to the harpoon like half-stunned bullocks to the knife; this horrid and indecent Right whaling, I say, compared to a spirited hunt for the gentlemanly Cachalot in southern and more genial seas, is as the butchery of white bears upon blank Greenland icebergs to zebra hunting in Caffraria, where the lively quarry bounds before you through leafy glades.

Herman Melville, *Mardi: and A Voyage Thither*, 1849

... for it was their custom, Mr Jonas said, whenever such a thing was practicable, to kill two birds with one stone, and never to throw away sprats, but as bait for whales.

Charles Dickens, *Martin Chuzzlewit*, 1843

COLLISION BETWEEN A STEAMER AND A WHALE.

Some Capricious Whale

I devoured with an avid eye the cotton wake which whitened the sea until lost from view! And how often have I shared the emotion of the top brass, of the crew, when some capricious whale raised its dark back above the waves! The deck of the vessel was crowded in a moment. The cabins poured forth a torrent of sailors and officers. Each one with heaving breath, with troubled eye, watching the course of the cetacean.

Jules Verne, *Twenty Thousand Leagues Under the Sea*, 1870

PINOCCHIO
and the
WHALE

Pinocchio swam faster and faster, and harder and harder.

'Faster, Pinocchio! The monster will get you! There he is! There he is! Quick, quick, or you are lost!'

Pinocchio went through the water like a shot – swifter and swifter. He came close to the rock. The Goat leaned over and gave him one of her hoofs to help him up out of the water. Alas! It was too late. The monster overtook him and the Marionette found himself in between the rows of gleaming white teeth. Only for a moment, however, for the Shark took a deep breath and, as he breathed, he drank in the Marionette as easily as he would have sucked an egg. Then he swallowed him so fast that Pinocchio, falling down into the body of the fish, lay stunned for a half hour.

When he recovered his senses the Marionette could not remember where he was. Around him all was darkness, a darkness so deep and so black that for a moment he thought he had put his head into an inkwell. He listened for a few moments and heard nothing. Once in a while a cold wind blew on his face. At first he could not understand where that wind was coming from, but after a while he understood that it came from the lungs of the monster. I forgot to tell you that the Shark was suffering from asthma, so that whenever he breathed a storm seemed to blow.

Carlo Collodi, *The Adventures of Pinocchio*, 1880

THE EYES OF A WHALE

… he had told none but absolutely true stories of foreign parts to the
neighbouring villagers when they saluted and clustered about him, as usual,
for anything he chose to pour forth — except that story of the whale whose eye
was about as large as the round pond in Derriman's ewe-lease — which was like
tempting fate to set a seal for ever upon his tongue as a traveller.

Thomas Hardy, *The Trumpet Major*, 1880

The Sea Wolf

O the blazing tropic night, when the wake's a welt of light
That holds the hot sky tame,
And the steady forefoot snores through the planet —
powdered floors
Where the scared whale flukes in flame.
Her plates are scarred by the sun, dear lass,
And her ropes are taut with the dew,
For we're booming down on the old trail, our own trail,
the out trail,
We're sagging south on the Long Trail —;
the trail that is
always new.

Jack London, *The Sea-Wolf*, 1904

A Whale! A Whale!

Jules Verne, *Robur the Conqueror*, 1886

The crew, as a change from the ordinary routine, would have endeavored to catch a few fish had there been any sign of them; but all that could be seen on the surface of the sea were a few of those yellow-bellied whales which measure about eighty feet in length. These are the most formidable cetaceans in the northern seas, and whalers are very careful in attacking them, for their strength is prodigious. However, in harpooning one of these whales, either with the ordinary harpoon, the Fletcher fuse, or the javelin-bomb, of which there was an assortment on board, there would have been danger to the men of the 'Albatross'.

But what was the good of such useless massacre? Doubtless to show off the powers of the aeronef to the members of the Weldon Institute. And so Robur gave orders for the capture of one of these monstrous cetaceans.

At the shout of 'A whale! A whale!' Uncle Prudent and Phil Evans came out of their cabin. Perhaps there was a whaler in sight! In that case all they had to do to escape from their flying prison was to jump into the sea, and chance being picked up by the vessel.

The crew were all on deck. 'Shall we try, sir?' asked Tom Turner.

'Yes', said Robur.

In the engine-room the engineer and his assistant were at their posts ready to obey the orders signaled to them. The 'Albatross' dropped towards the sea, and remained, about fifty feet above it.

There was no ship in sight — of that the two colleagues soon assured themselves — nor was there any land to be seen to which they could swim, providing Robur made no attempt to recapture them.

Several jets of water from the spout holes soon announced the presence of the whales as they came to the surface to breathe. Tom Turner and one of the men were in the bow. Within his reach was one of those javelin-bombs, of Californian make, which are shot from an arquebus and which are shaped as a metallic cylinder terminated by a cylindrical shell armed with a shaft having a barbed point. Robur was a little farther aft, and with his right hand signaled to the engineers, while with his left, he directed the steersman. He thus controlled the aeronef in every way, horizontally and vertically, and it is almost impossible to conceive with what speed and precision the 'Albatross' answered to his orders. She seemed a living being, of which he was the soul.

'A whale! A whale!' shouted Tom Turner, as the back of a cetacean emerged from the surface about four cable-lengths in front of the 'Albatross'.

The 'Albatross' swept towards it, and when she was within sixty feet of it she stopped dead.

Tom Turner seized the arquebus, which was resting against a cleat on the rail. He fired, and the projectile, attached to a long line, entered the whale's body. The shell, filled with an explosive compound, burst, and shot out a small harpoon with two branches, which fastened into the animal's flesh.

'Look out!' shouted Turner.

Uncle Prudent and Phil Evans, much against their will, became greatly interested in the spectacle.

The whale, seriously wounded, gave the sea such a slap with his tail, that the water dashed up over the bow of the aeronef. Then he plunged to a great depth, while the line, which had been previously wetted in a tub of water to prevent its taking fire, ran out like lightning. When the whale rose to the surface he started off at full speed in a northerly direction.

It may be imagined with what speed the 'Albatross' was towed in pursuit. Besides, the propellers had been stopped. The whale was let go as he would, and the ship followed him. Turner stood ready to cut the line in case a fresh plunge should render this towing dangerous.

For half an hour, and perhaps for a distance of six miles, the 'Albatross' was thus dragged along, but it was obvious that the whale was tiring. Then, at a gesture from Robur the assistant engineers started the propellers astern, so as to oppose a certain resistance to the whale, who was gradually getting closer.

Soon the aeronef was gliding about twenty-five feet above him. His tail was beating the waters with incredible violence, and as he turned over on his back an enormous wave was produced.

Suddenly the whale turned up again, so as to take a header, as it were, and then dived with such rapidity that Turner had barely time to cut the line.

The aeronef was dragged to the very surface of the water. A whirlpool was formed where the animal had disappeared. A wave dashed up on to the deck as if the aeronef were a ship driving against wind and tide.

Luckily, with a blow of the hatchet the mate severed the line, and the 'Albatross', freed from her tug, sprang aloft six hundred feet under the impulse of her ascensional screws. Robur had maneuvered his ship without losing his coolness for a moment.

A few minutes afterwards the whale returned to the surface — dead. From every side the birds flew down on to the carcass, and their cries were enough to deafen a congress. The 'Albatross', without stopping to share in the spoil, resumed her course to the west.

WHALES *Weep* NOT

D. H. *Lawrence, 1932*

They say the sea is cold, but the sea contains
the hottest blood of all, and the wildest, the most urgent.

All the whales in the wider deeps, hot are they, as they urge
on and on, and dive beneath the icebergs.
The right whales, the sperm-whales, the hammer-heads, the killers
there they blow, there they blow, hot wild white breath out of the sea!

And they rock, and they rock, through the sensual ageless ages
on the depths of the seven seas,
and through the salt they reel with drunk delight
and in the tropics tremble they with love
and roll with massive, strong desire, like gods.
Then the great bull lies up against his bride
in the blue deep bed of the sea,
as mountain pressing on mountain, in the zest of life:
and out of the inward roaring of the inner red ocean of whale-blood
the long tip reaches strong, intense, like the maelstrom-tip, and comes to rest
in the clasp and the soft, wild clutch of a she-whale's fathomless body.

And over the bridge of the whale's strong phallus, linking the wonder of whales
the burning archangels under the sea keep passing, back and forth,
keep passing, archangels of bliss
from him to her, from her to him, great Cherubim
that wait on whales in mid-ocean, suspended in the waves of the sea
great heaven of whales in the waters, old hierarchies.

And enormous mother whales lie dreaming suckling their whale-tender young
and dreaming with strange whale eyes wide open in the waters of the beginning
and the end.

And bull-whales gather their women and whale-calves in a ring
when danger threatens, on the surface of the ceaseless flood
and range themselves like great fierce Seraphim facing the threat
encircling their huddled monsters of love.
And all this happens in the sea, in the salt
where God is also love, but without words:
and Aphrodite is the wife of whales
most happy, happy she!

and Venus among the fishes skips and is a she-dolphin
she is the gay, delighted porpoise sporting with love and the sea
she is the female tunny-fish, round and happy among the males
and dense with happy blood, dark rainbow bliss in the sea.

This is the flower that smiles on every one,
To show his teeth as white as whale's bone;

Shakespeare, *Love's Labours Lost*, c.1595–96

There was no life there. It was inchoate and diffuse, extending for
many square acres and then fringing off into the void. No, it was
not life. But might it not be the remains of life? Above all, might it
not be the food of life, of monstrous life, even as the humble grease
of the ocean is the food for the mighty whale?

A. Conan Doyle, *The Black Doctor*, 1919

Nothing but sky appears, so close the root
And grass of the hill-top level with the air—
Blue sunny air, where a great cloud floats, laden
With light, like a dead whale that white birds pick,
Floating away in the sun in some north sea.

Robert Browning, 'Pauline', 1833

Sprats, Whales
and Dog-fish

Joseph Conrad, *The Secret Agent*, 1907

'Do you know what may be done with a sprat?' the Assistant Commissioner asked in his turn.

'He's sometimes put into a sardine box,' chuckled Toodles, whose erudition on the subject of the fishing industry was fresh and, in comparison with his ignorance of all other industrial matters, immense. 'There are sardine canneries on the Spanish coast which—'

The Assistant Commissioner interrupted the apprentice statesman.

'Yes. Yes. But a sprat is also thrown away sometimes in order to catch a whale.'

'A whale. Phew!' exclaimed Toodles, with bated breath. 'You're after a whale, then?'

'Not exactly. What I am after is more like a dog-fish. You don't know perhaps what a dog-fish is like.'

'Yes; I do. We're buried in special books up to our necks — whole shelves full of them — with plates … It's a noxious, rascally looking, altogether detestable beast, with a sort of smooth face and moustaches.'

'Described to a T,' commended the Assistant Commissioner. 'Only mine is clean-shaven altogether. You've seen him. It's a witty fish.'

THE FORSAKEN MERMAN

༄

CHILDREN DEAR, WAS IT YESTERDAY

WE HEARD THE SWEET BELLS OVER THE BAY?

IN THE CAVERNS WHERE WE LAY,

THROUGH THE SURF AND THROUGH THE SWELL,

THE FAR-OFF SOUND OF A SILVER BELL?

SAND-STREWN CAVERNS, COOL AND DEEP,

WHERE THE WINDS ARE ALL ASLEEP;

WHERE THE SPENT LIGHTS QUIVER AND GLEAM,

WHERE THE SALT WEED SWAYS IN THE STREAM,

WHERE THE SEA-BEASTS, RANGED ALL ROUND,

FEED IN THE OOZE OF THEIR PASTURE-GROUND;

WHERE THE SEA-SNAKES COIL AND TWINE,

DRY THEIR MAIL AND BASK IN THE BRINE;

WHERE GREAT WHALES COME SAILING BY,

SAIL AND SAIL, WITH UNSHUT EYE,

ROUND THE WORLD FOR EVER AND AYE?

WHEN DID MUSIC COME THIS WAY?

CHILDREN DEAR, WAS IT YESTERDAY?

༄

Matthew Arnold,
'The Forsaken Merman', 1849

THE WELLFLEET WHALE

STANLEY KUNITZ, 1983

You have your language too,
an eerie medley of clicks
and hoots and trills,
location-notes and love calls,
whistles and grunts. Occasionally,
it's like furniture being smashed,
or the creaking of a mossy door,
sounds that all melt into a liquid
song with endless variations,
as if to compensate
for the vast loneliness of the sea.
Sometimes a disembodied voice
breaks in, as if from distant reefs,
and it's as much as one can bear
to listen to its long mournful cry,
a sorrow without name, both more
and less than human. It drags
across the ear like a record
running down.

No wind. No waves. No clouds.
Only the whisper of the tide,
as it withdrew, stroking the shore,
a lazy drift of gulls overhead,
and tiny points of light
bubbling in the channel.
It was the tag-end of summer.
From the harbor's mouth
you coasted into sight,
flashing news of your advent,
the crescent of your dorsal fin
clipping the diamonded surface.
We cheered at the sign of your greatness
when the black barrel of your head
erupted, ramming the water,

and you flowered for us
in the jet of your spouting.
All afternoon you swam
tirelessly round the bay,
with such an easy motion,
the slightest downbeat of your tail,
an almost imperceptible
undulation of your flippers,
you seemed like something poured,
not driven; you seemed
to marry grace with power.
And when you bounded into air,
slapping your flukes,
we thrilled to look upon
pure energy incarnate
as nobility of form.
You seemed to ask of us
not sympathy, or love,
or understanding,
but awe and wonder.

That night we watched you
swimming in the moon.
Your back was molten silver.
We guessed your silent passage
by the phosphorescence in your wake.
At dawn we found you stranded on the rocks.

There came a boy and a man
and yet other men running, and two
schoolgirls in yellow halters
and a housewife bedecked
with curlers, and whole families in beach
buggies with assorted yelping dogs.
The tide was almost out.

That night
watched you
swimming i
moon.
Your back
molten silve
We guessed y
silent passa
by the
phosphores
your wake.
At dawn w
you strande
rocks.

THE idea OF MIRACLE THE WHALES COMPANION

We could walk around you,
as you heaved deeper into the shoal,
crushed by your own weight,
collapsing into yourself,
your flippers and your flukes
quivering, your blowhole
spasmodically bubbling, roaring.
In the pit of your gaping mouth
you bared your fringework of baleen,
a thicket of horned bristles.
When the Curator of Mammals
arrived from Boston
to take samples of your blood
you were already oozing from below.
Somebody had carved his initials
in your flank. Hunters of souvenirs
had peeled off strips of your skin,
a membrane thin as paper.
You were blistered and cracked by the sun.
The gulls had been pecking at you.
The sound you made was a hoarse and fitful bleating.

What drew us to the magnet of your dying?
You made a bond between us,
the keepers of the nightfall watch,
who gathered in a ring around you,
boozing in the bonfire light.
Toward dawn we shared with you
your hour of desolation,
the huge lingering passion
of your unearthly outcry,
as you swung your blind head
toward us and laboriously opened
a bloodshot, glistening eye,
in which we swam with terror and recognition.

That night we
watched you
swimming in th
moon.
Your back was
molten silver.
We guessed your
silent passage
by the

Voyager, chief of the pelagic world,
you brought with you the myth
of another country, dimly remembered,
where flying reptiles
lumbered over the steaming marshes
and trumpeting thunder lizards
wallowed in the reeds.
While empires rose and fell on land,
your nation breasted the open main,
rocked in the consoling rhythm
of the tides. Which ancestor first plunged
head-down through zones of colored twilight
to scour the bottom of the dark?
You ranged the North Atlantic track
from Port-of-Spain to Baffin Bay,
edging between the ice-floes
through the fat of summer,
lob-tailing, breaching, sounding,
grazing in the pastures of the sea
on krill-rich orange plankton
crackling with life.
You prowled down the continental shelf,
guided by the sun and stars
and the taste of alluvial silt
on your way southward
to the warm lagoons,
the tropic of desire,
where the lovers lie belly to belly
in the rub and nuzzle of the sporting;
and you turned, like a god in exile,
out of your wide primeval element,
delivered to the mercy of time.
Master of the whale-roads,
let the white wings of the gulls
spread out their cover.
You have become like us,
disgraced and mortal.

That night watched you
swimming in moon.
Your back molten silve
We guessed y
silent passa
by the
phosphores
your wake.
At dawn we
you strande
rocks.

Chapter **4**

THERE *she* BLOWS!

Hunting the whale

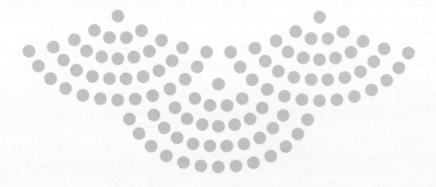

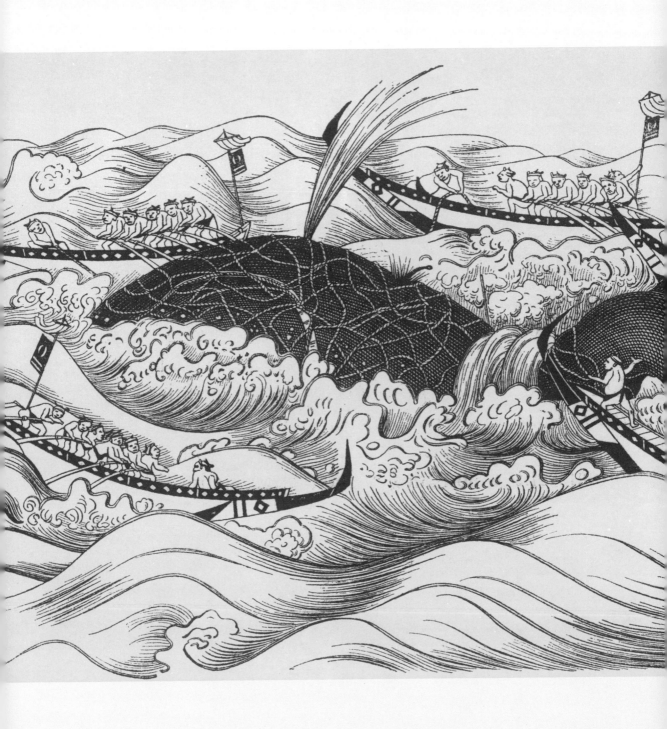

The hunted whale is an image that conjures up a range of emotions, from sadness and anger, to excitement and fear. Once the sight of a whale's blowhole would have meant great joy to a the crew of a Nantucket whaling vessel, as one whale represented half a year's wages — a far cry from the modern ocean-gazer's delight at the prospect of a breaching whale. It is interesting that R. M. Ballantyne notes that there are few things in this world more astonishing than 'that a man can kill a whale'. The modern reader probably assumes this is an environmental statement, but actually it's just amazement that humans can successfully tackle and kill such a huge beast, which was generally considered by the whaler as 'gold within his grasp' — particularly as almost every part of the whale could be sold and used for some purpose, whether oil for candles or bones for corsets. However, life on board a whaler was tough, with whalers often being at sea for months before even seeing a whale, let alone catching one. The whaling industry of the nineteenth century was a thriving business, but it wasn't until the twentieth century, where modern boats could catch a whale a day, that extinction became a serious concern.

Enticed by the riches that would come from vanquishing whales, man disturbed the peace of their vast wilderness, violated their haven, wiped out all those unable to steal away to the inaccessible wasteland of icy polar seas ... and so, the giant of giants fell prey to his weaponry. Since man shall never change, only when they cease to exist shall these enormous species cease to be the victims of his self interest. They flee before him, but it is no use; man's resourcefulness transports him to the ends of the earth. Death is their only refuge now.

Bernard Germaine Lacépède, 1804

Gold *within his* grasp
The ocean, not to be behindhand with the
earth, yielded up her mighty whales, that
Mr Gathergold might sell their oil, and make
a profit of it. Be the original commodity what
it might, it was gold within his grasp.

Nathaniel Hawthorne, *The Great Stone Face*, 1850

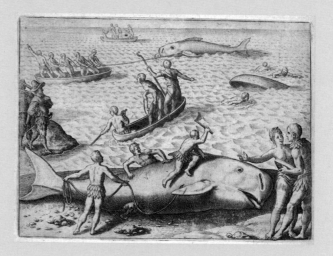

Man versus whale

There are few things in this world that have filled me with so much astonishment as
the fact that man can kill a whale! That a fish, more than sixty feet long, and thirty
feet round the body; with the bulk of three hundred fat oxen rolled into one; with
the strength of many hundreds of horses; able to swim at a rate that would carry
it right round the world in twenty-three days; that can smash a boat to atoms with
one slap of its tail, and stave in the planks of a ship with one blow of its thick skull;
— that such a monster can be caught and killed by man, is most wonderful to hear
of, but I can tell from experience that it is much more wonderful to see.

R. M. Ballantyne, *Fighting the Whales*, 1915

THE WHALE-SHIP W. H. G. Kingston, *Peter the Whaler*, 1851

A whaler, in order to withstand the shock of the ice, is strengthened inside, both at the stem and stern, by stout timbers placed in various directions, and fastened securely together; while on the outside she is in parts covered with a double, and even a treble planking, besides other thick pieces, which serve to ward off the blows from the parts most likely to receive them. How little all the strengthening which the art and ingenuity of man can devise is of avail against the mighty power of the ice, I shall have hereafter to describe. The masts of a whaler are lower than in a common merchantman, and her sails are smaller, and cut in a different shape, the courses or lower sails decreasing towards the foot, so as to be worked with slight strength. Sometimes this is of importance, as, when all the boats are away together in chase of whales, three or four men alone remain on board to take care of the ship.

A whale-ship, therefore, though she has great care and expense bestowed on her, has not, in port, the graceful and elegant appearance possessed by some other ships, bound to more genial climes. The crew do not sleep in hammocks, as on board men-of-war, but in berths or standing bed-places, erected on the half-deck forward. It is a dark retreat, and not scented with sweet odours, especially after a ship has begun to take in her cargo; but the weary seaman cares little where he lays his head, provided it is in a dry and warm place.

We next come to the boats — a very important part of the outfit. The bow and stern of a whale-boat are both sharp, rise considerably, and are nearly alike. It has great beam, or breadth, to prevent its being dragged, when towed by a whale, completely under the water. The keel is convex in the centre, to enable it to be turned more easily; and for the same reason it is steered by an oar instead of a rudder. The oar can also turn a boat when she is at rest, and can scull her in calm weather up to a whale without noise. A large-size boat is pulled by five oars, and one to steer, and a small one by four oars; the first being from twenty-six to twenty-eight feet long, and the last from twenty-three to twenty-four. A large one is five feet five inches in breadth; and a small one five feet three inches.

The rowers include the harpooner and the line-manager. They are carvel-built — that is, the planks are placed as in a ship. Boats in general are clinker-built — that is, the planks overlap each other; but as they are difficult to repair, the other simpler method is employed. A ship generally carries seven boats — two or more large, and the rest small. They are suspended by cranes, or davits, in a row outside the rigging, on either side of the ship, and another astern, so that they can be directly lowered into the water. A smart crew will man and lower a boat in the space of a minute, and be away in chase of a whale.

GLOSSARY OF WHALING TERMS

AMBERGRIS, a substance found in the throat of, usually, a sick whale. Used in the perfume industry and worth more than gold.

BAILER, a long handled dipper made of copper for removing the hot oil from the trypots.

BAILING, the act of removing the spermaceti from the head or case of the sperm whale.

BALEEN, the black whalebone that comes from the mouths of toothless whales.

BALEEN WHALES, all whales except sperm or toothed whales.

BARRELS, the unit of measure for whale oil. 31½ Imperial Gallons = 1 Barrel

BIBLE LEAVES, when the blubber has been flensed from the whale it was lowered into the blubber room where it was cut into manageable strips called 'horse pieces'. These were then sliced into thin pieces called 'bible leaves'. Cutting the blubber into thin strips made it easier to boil the blubber and extract the oil.

BLACKFISH, a small whale, also known as a Pilot Whale. The raised forehead or 'melon' gave the finest known lubricant when boiled out.

BLACKSKIN, the thin and slimy outer covering of the whales blubber. It is so tender it can easily be scraped off with a finger nail.

BLANKET PIECE, as the whale is being flensed, the spademen stand on the cutting-in stage and slice the blubber as it is being hauled on board. The blubber is peeled off in a continuous strip, much like peeling an orange.

BLOW, a spout. The moist visible breath of a whale.

BLOWS, 'There she blows', the lookouts call to alert those on deck.

BLUBBER, the skin and fatty sublayer of the whale, usually 12 to 18 inches thick.

BLUBBER GAFF, a short handled hook for dragging the blubber around the decks.

BLUBBER HOOK, an iron hook, about 100 lbs in weight hanging from the cutting tackle for hoisting the blubber on board.

BLUBBER ROOM, a space in the hold near the main hatch used for the temporary storage of blubber.

BLUE WHALE, the largest animal on earth and known to the whalers as sulpher-bottom. Not normally taken by the sailing whalers as the carcase sinks almost immediately the whale dies.

BOATS CREW, normally six men, Mate in charge, boatsteerer and four pulling hands.

BOATSTEERER, an experienced seaman who rows the bow oar and when 'on the whale' throws the harpoon and fastens to the whale. The mate then takes over to lance and kill the whale.

BULL, the large male whale.

BURGOO, the seamans name for a porridge dish made of oatmeal, even the worst cook could make burgoo.

CACHALOT, the French name for whales.

CAMBOOSE, the galley deckhouse, also known as caboose, from the term cab-house. Usually sited between the main and mizzen masts.

CASE, the space in the sperm whales skull, containing about 500 gallons of the finest oil.

COOLER, an iron tank into which the hot oil is firstly poured for cooling before stowing below.

CUTTING IN, the act of stripping the blubber from the whale carcase.

CUTTING IN STAGE, this was a three sided platform projecting over the starboard side of the ship, amidships, on which the captain and a mate would stand with their cutting spades to flense the whale.

DART, this iron, or harpoon was thin and razor sharp

and had no line attached. It was socketed into a wooden shaft and when thrown correctly would penetrate into the whales lungs and cause death.

DARTING, the act of throwing the iron into the whale. Normally thrown by the mate.

DAVITS, the whaleboats hung from the davits ready for instant lowering. Usually there were four pairs of davits and they were fitted two forward and two aft, port and starboard.

DONKEYS BREAKFAST, the sailors straw filled hessian mattress, home to a million bedbugs.

FLENSING, the act of cutting the blubber from the whale.

FLUKES, the whale's tail. On a fully grown sperm whale it could be up to 21 feet across.

FLUKE CHAIN, the chain strop shackled around the tail to hold the whale alongside.

FLURRY, the final moments of a whales life after it has been lanced.

GALLIED, the whaleman's term for a spooked or frightened whale.

GAMMING, when two or more whaling ships met at sea, generally they would stop, lower boats and visit each other to have a 'gam' and catch up on the latest news.

GRAMPUS, a small variety of whale which make a grunting noise when they blow.

GREENHAND, an inexperienced man on his first whaling cruise.

HARDTACK, ship's biscuit baked very hard to resist deterioration.

HARPING IRON, the original name for the harpoon.

HARPOON, the first iron to strike the whale. This is a modern term and was not used by the sailing whalers.

HORSE PIECES, blubber cut to a convenient size for handling in the blubber room.

HUMPBACK WHALE, an inshore whale, not often taken by the sailing whalers because it sank when dead.

IRON, the whaleman's name for the harpoon. 'Sinking the iron' was the act of striking the whale. The iron, a spear with a single razor sharp barb, had the line attached which was coiled in the line tub. Normally thrown by the boatsteerer.

LANCE, also known as the **DART,** this was the killing spear thrown by the mate.

LARBOARD, an archaic term denoting the left or port side of the ship.

LAY THE BOAT ON, to direct the boat onto the whale in the most advantageous position for darting.

LINE TUB, a large shallow wooden tub in which the whale line is coiled. Two tubs to each boat.

LOBSCOUSE, a common dish cooked on the whalers. It was made from salt beef and a hash made from hardtack and fat to which soaked pease was added.

LOGGERHEAD, a square piece of timber standing vertically from the stern of the whaleboat and around which the whaleline is snubbed.

POD, the common name for a school, herd or shoal of whales.

RAISE WHALES, to sight the whales or their blows and announce it to the deck.

RIGHT WHALE, is the baleen whale of temperate waters. He has no hump and is smooth bellied.

RUN, to, the act of the whale when gallied or frightened. Whales don't swim, they run, sound settle, bolt, breach or round to.

SCHOOLMASTER, a large bull whale predominant in the pod.

SCRAP, blubber from which the oil has been boiled out. When semi-dried it becomes fuel for the tryworks.

SCRIMSHAW, the art of the whaleman. Usually pictures

of their ships drawn on the whales teeth, but also carved ornamental work and busks.

SEA PIG, the whalers name for the porpoise. They were harpooned to provide fresh meat during the voyage.

SOUNDING, the whales, after breathing on the surface go deep and this is known as sounding.

SPADES, the cutting tools used by men on the cutting stage to remove the blubber in blanket pieces.

SPEAK TO, to hail a ship by voice or flag signals indicating that you wish to speak to them.

SPERMACETTI, the whalemans term for the sperm whale, also the case or head matter of the sperm whale.

STERN ALL, the order given when the whale has been ironed. To back away in a hurry.

STOVE, to be, this term refers to the smashing of the whaleboat, usually by the whale's tail as it threshes after being ironed. Sometimes the whale will attack the boat with its jaw and bite the boat in two.

STRIKE, to get fast to the whale.

SULPHER BOTTOM, the whaleman's name for the great rorqual or blue whale.

TACKLE, to, to close with and get ready to iron the whale.

TAKE, the, the total amount of oil and bone taken during the cruise.

TAKE THE LINE, the whale has run and taken all the line out of the two tubs.

THERE SHE BLOWS, this is the common announcement made by the lookout when he first sights the whales spouts. This was followed by the mates, 'WHERE AWAY', The lookout would then indicate by arm signal and voice where the whales were to be found.

TRYWORKS, a brick built structure sited between the fore and main masts. It was about 10 feet by 8 feet by 5 feet high. It was built on special strengthening beams and secured to the deck with iron angles. The structure contained two large iron pots in which the blubber pieces were boiled. The fires were started with wood and once lit were fed with pieces of blubber already tried out. Underneath the fire grates was a deep trough filled with water to prevent the decks from catching alight.

TRYING OUT, the act of boiling the oil from the blubber.

WAIF POLE, a pole that had a flag attached. It was used for 'marking' killed floating whales so that the boat could go on and chase others and then come back and collect the marked one.

WHALEBONE, the black fibrous bone from the right whale.

WHALELINE, the rope leading from the line tub to the harpoon.

WHALEMAN, a term that applied to a man that had completed at least one full cruise on a whaleship.

WHERE AWAY, the officers response to the cry of **THERE SHE BLOWS**.

WOOD TO BLACKSKIN, the term that is used when the stern of the whaleboat collides with the skin of the whale when the boat is laying on to either iron or lance the whale.

Captain Thomas Dennis, *To King George III Sound for Whales, 1800–1802*

Whalers' wages

On an average a whale is worth £400. A tenth of this goes to the captain, that is £40; the first officer receives a fortieth, £10; the other officers a sixtieth, from £6 to £7; while the members of the crew draw from a two-hundredth to a two-hundred-and-fortieth, say from 33/- to 40/- approximately. As the fishing payment is not by the month, but by a share, it is calculated proportionately for each one according to the terms of the contract, the number of gallons of oil obtained during the cruise, and the price the oil realizes at Havre at the moment of its sale or delivery.

Dr Felix Maynard and Alexandre Dumas, *The Whalers*, 1859

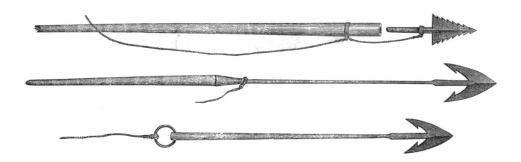

Catching a whale

It is a risky business catching a whale. It's safer for me to go on the river with my boat, than to go hunting whales with many boats ... I prefer to catch a fish that I can kill, rather than a fish that can sink or kill not only me but also my companions with a single blow.

Aelfric, *Colloquy*, c.990

Danger, toil and suffering

Their lives have ever been one continual round of hair-breadth escapes … Many a tale of danger and toil and suffering, startling, severe, and horrible, has illumined the pages of the history of this pursuit, and scarce any, even the humblest of these hardy mariners, but can, from his own experience, narrate truths stranger than fiction.

Alexander Starbuck, *History of the American Whale Fishery*, 1877

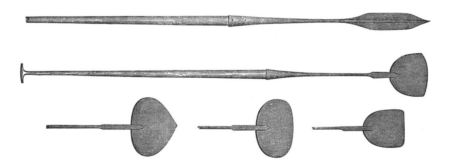

NO BRAVER OR GAMIER MEN

Whalemen enjoyed a variety of adventures such as no other calling approached, such as no millionaire big-game hunter of to-day can command. Not the raw recruit, marching from the bosom of his wife into the fever heat of his first battle; not the dead man's ghost encountering the first unknown phantom in the other world; — neither of these can feel stranger and stronger emotions than that man does, who for the first time finds himself pulling into the charmed churned circle of the hunted sperm whale. When that moment came, no braver or gamier men could be found on blue water, than the whalemen of New England.

Samuel Eliot Morison, *The Maritime History of Massachusetts 1783–1860*, 1921

THE SLAUGHTER

A whaler's journal

There was a time, (so says my rhyme,
And so 'tis prosed by many)
Sperm whales were found on 'Japan Ground,'
But now there are not any.

Oh, whales! Sperm Whales!
Come, pray come!
And assist a gallant crew
Who are watching here for you
To a thousand barrels more.
Then, gales! Sweet gales!
Come, pray, come! —
Ev'ry cloth shall woo the breeze,
While it bears us o'er the seas,
To our dearest native shore,
To our home, 'Sweet home'!

August! thou has not kindly been
To us lone wand'ring whaling-men:
Thou'st ta'en away from us the whales,
And left us, in their stead, strong gales,
Rough seas and squalls, and rain.
Let me invoke thy end may savour
Of winds and weather more in favour, —

That thy departing days may bring
(The oil to which our hopes did cling)
Two hundred barrels gain!

Thankful we are for what we do receive,
But when we've nought, we're very prone to grieve: —
Give us, this season, but Five Hundred more,
Our thanks shall swell above old Ocean's roar.

Here let me fervently our thanks express:
Indeed we're thankful for this day's success.
Hope dawns again, and bids us cease to sorrow.
O, may we take a couple more tomorrow!

Sperm Oil! Sperm Oil! —
By patient toil our eighteenth hundred's o'er —
Reader, conceive how much we grieve to want seven hundred more.
Sweep us, sweet gales, among sperm whales,
till all our casks o'erflow —
Then swell the breeze, and far o'er seas our gallant bark shall go.
Haste, Time! Oh, haste! and let us taste a kindly welcome home
By those we love — and to them prove no more the main we'll roam.

An anonymous journal keeper on the *Elizabeth*, 1837

Poor ANTONE

December 28. Saw whales just before breakfast; immediately after breakfast lowered the boats. Mr. Nickerson's boat soon got fast to one, when he capsized the boat and precipitated them all in the water. Mr. St. John with the waist boat immediately went to their rescue, but before he reached them, one poor fellow had found a watery grave. He said he could not swim, so Mr. Nickerson gave him an oar that he might keep himself up, but we think he must have had the cramp and let go his hold on the oar.

Poor Antone! He came out as one of the cabin boys and had lived in the cabin for a year and then at his own request went to live in the forecastle. He was so anxious to go out in a boat after whales. He was a smart, active boy of eighteen years, and I had posed to Samuel that we should take him home with us and give him the benefit of a little education. That was a sad day for us, Antone, when thou wast summoned into the mysteries of the unseen world without a moment's warning. May God in his infinite goodness have mercy on thy soul.

In the afternoon saw whales again, lowered the boats, and Mr. Chappell struck one which they soon killed. Commenced cutting in about half-past three; finished at 11 p.m. The sad events of the day had made me almost sick, so I took a cup of tea by myself and went early to bed.

The Captain's Best Mate: The Journal of Mary Chipman Lawrence on the Whaler Addison, 1856–1860

The wager

All ye mast-headers have before now heard me give orders about a white whale. Look ye! d'ye see this Spanish ounce of gold? ... it is a sixteen-dollar piece, men ... Whosoever of ye raises me a white-headed whale with a wrinkled brow and a crooked jaw; whosoever of ye raises me that white-headed whale, with three holes punctured in his starboard fluke — look ye, whosoever of ye raises me that same white whale, he shall have this gold ounce, my boys!

Herman Melville, *Moby Dick*, 1851

Catching horse whales

He visited this country also with a view of catching horse-whales, which had bones of very great value for their teeth, of which he brought some to the king ... The best whales were catched in his own country, of which some were forty-eight, some fifty yards long. He said that he was one of six who had killed sixty in two days.

Octher's verbal narrative taken down from his mouth by King Alfred, AD 890

Luring a Whale

Cetus, a whale is the largest of all fish. He has a big, wide mouth. He spouts water into the air like clouds, so that he often sinks ships, and he grows so large that no man can catch him. But if the fishers know where the whale is hiding out, they come together with many ships. Then they have flutes on which they play tunefully and they give shrill blasts on the trumpets and with that sound they lure the whale. He comes close to the ships to hear that music and lies on the surface with his back above the water. Then they have a curved instrument with iron teeth like a saw that they throw vigorously into the back, after which they slip away as stealthily and quietly as they can. Not long afterwards he feels the wound and sinks to the seabed, where he wants to rub his back against the bed, but in doing so he drives the iron even deeper into the wound so that it penetrates the layer of fat, touches the flesh, and finally reaches the innermost part of his body. The iron enters the wound with the salt water and kills the whale. When he is dead, he floats up to the surface of the sea again and the fishers return and tie him tightly with large canvases and ropes and bring him joyfully to land.

Adriaen Coenen, *The Whale Book*, 1585

Thar *she* blows

❧

OCTOBER 13. 'THERE SHE BLOWS',

WAS SUNG OUT FROM THE MAST-HEAD.

'WHERE AWAY?' DEMANDED THE CAPTAIN.

'THREE POINTS OFF THE LEE BOW, SIR.'

'RAISE UP YOUR WHEEL. STEADY!'

'STEADY, SIR.'

'MAST-HEAD AHOY! DO YOU SEE THAT WHALE NOW?'

'AY, AY, SIR! A SHOAL OF SPERM WHALES!

THERE SHE BLOWS! THERE SHE BREACHES!'

'SING OUT! SING OUT EVERY TIME!'

'AY AY, SIR! THERE SHE BLOWS!

THERE — THERE — THAR SHE BLOWS — BOWES — BO-O-O-S!'

'HOW FAR OFF?' 'TWO MILES AND A HALF.'

'THUNDER AND LIGHTNING! SO NEAR! CALL ALL HANDS.'

❧

J. Ross Browne, *Etchings of a Whaling Cruise*, 1846

MARSEILLE. — Transport d'une baleine capturée dans les eaux du château d'If. — D'après un croquis de M. B. Landais.

BOLDHEART! BOLDHEART!

Charles Dickens, *Holiday Romance*, 1868

It was under these circumstances that the look-out at the masthead gave the word, 'Whales!'

All was now activity.

'Where away?' cried Capt. Boldheart, starting up.

'On the larboard bow, sir', replied the fellow at the masthead, touching his hat. For such was the height of discipline on board of 'The Beauty', that, even at that height, he was obliged to mind it, or be shot through the head.

'This adventure belongs to me', said Boldheart. 'Boy, my harpoon. Let no man follow'; and leaping alone into his boat, the captain rowed with admirable dexterity in the direction of the monster.

All was now excitement.

'He nears him!' said an elderly seaman, following the captain through his spy-glass.

'He strikes him!' said another seaman, a mere stripling, but also with a spy-glass.

'He tows him towards us!' said another seaman, a man in the full vigour of life, but also with a spy-glass.

In fact, the captain was seen approaching, with the huge bulk following. We will not dwell on the deafening cries of 'Boldheart! Boldheart!' with which he was received, when, carelessly leaping on the quarter-deck, he presented his prize to his men. They afterwards made two thousand four hundred and seventeen pound ten and sixpence by it.

A raal oil-butt, that fellow!

'I rather conclude, sir', said the cockswain rolling over his tobacco in his mouth, very composedly, while his little sunken eyes began to twinkle with pleasure at the sight, 'the gentleman has lost his reckoning, and don't know which way to head, to take himself back into blue water'.

'Tis a fin-back!' exclaimed the lieutenant; 'he will soon make head-way, and be off'.

'No, Sir, 'tis a Right Whale', answered Tom; 'I saw his sprout; he threw up a pair of as pretty rainbows as a Christian would wish to look at. He's a raal oil-butt, that fellow!'

James Fenimore Cooper, *The Pilot*, 1806

THE GREENLAND Whale Fishery

I can no longer stop on shore
Since I am so deep in debt
So a voyage to Greenland I must go
Some money for to get Brave Boys

Now Greenland it is a very cold coast
There is nothing but frost and snow
But it is the place likewise my boys
Where the whale fish blows Brave Boys

Our Chief Mate was at the main mast head
With a spy glass in his hand
Here's a whale, a whale, a whale fish he cries
And she blows at every span Brave Boys

Our Captain was on the quarter deck
And a very good man was he
Overhaul overhaul your davit tackle falls
And launch your boats to sea Brave Boys

Now the boats being lowered and all were manned
Resolved was each boat's crew
For to steer to sail to paddle and to row
To the place where the whale fish blows Brave Boys

Now the whale being struck and the line paid out
O he gave a splash with his tail
He capsized the boat and we lost five men
Nor did we get that whale Brave Boys

Now when the news to our Captain came
He called up all his crew
For the losing of these five brave men
He down his colors drew Brave Boys

Now the losing of the five brave men
Did grieve his heart full sore
But the losing of the fine Rite whale
It grieved him a damd sight more Brave Boys

A SURE PRIZE

The monster leaps out of the sea, flourishing her tail and fins, and strikes the water with a noise as loud as cannon. She wriggles, and plunges, and twists more furiously than ever, and splashes blood over the boat's crew, who still restrain their excitement, and remain collected in all that they do. She is now in her 'flurry' — she is said to 'spout thick blood', and is a sure prize. The boat, by great good management, escapes all accident, and the headsman chuckles as he cuts a notch on the logger-head, and gives the crew a 'tot all round', promising the novice that he will have to treat the party to a gallon to-night, in order to pay his footing on killing his first fish.

Oliver Goldsmith, *A History of Earth and Animated Nature*, 1774

Planting the harpoon

Most landlubbers suppose — as I did formerly — that a Yankee whaleman captures his prey by maneuvering the boat somewhere near the whale and then throwing the harpoon at it. Nothing of the sort! The harpoon is not 'thrown'; it is planted. It rarely leaves the hands of the boatsteerer until the boat has been beached on the whale's back. 'Wood to blackskin', is the muttered or grunted order by which the boatheader holds his harponeer's eagerness in check while the craft is sailing, or being pulled, onto the whale.

Robert Cushman, *Logbook for Grace: Whaling Brig Daisy*, 1912–1913

Perils of Whaling.

THE STORMBEATEN WIDOWER'S LIFE

As is frequently the case among the whalers
of Martha's Vineyard, so much of this
stormbeaten widower's life had been tossed
away on distant seas, that out of twenty years of
matrimony he had spent scarce three, and those
at scattered intervals, beneath his own roof.

Nathaniel Hawthorne, 'Chippings with a Chisel',
Twice-Told Tales, 1837

SPOUT! SPOUT! SPOUT!

THE WAVES ARE PURLING ALL ABOUT,

EVERY BILLOW ON ITS HEAD

STRANGELY WEARS A CREST OF RED.

SEE HER LASH THE FOAMING MAIN

IN HER FLURRY AND HER PAIN.

TAKE GOOD HEED, MY HEARTS OF OAK,

LEST HER FLUKES, AS SHE LIES,

SWIFTLY HURL YOU TO THE SKIES.

BUT LO! HER GIANT STRENGTH IS BROKE.

SLOW SHE TURNS, AS A MASS OF LEAD;

THE MIGHTY MOUNTAIN WHALE IS DEAD.

Anonymous whaler's song, 19th century

HALEY'S *first* WHALE

WE HAD JUST FINISHED SUPPER and lit our pipes, when the man at the masthead sung out:

'School of sperm whales on the lee beam, not half a mile off!'

Casting our eyes in that direction, we could see twenty or thirty good-sized whales tumbling about when the big seas would catch them and almost turn them over. Sometimes one could be seen on the crest of a wave. As it broke he would shoot down its side with such speed a streak of white could be seen in the wake he made through the water. When reaching the hollow between two seas he would lazily shove his spout holes above water and blow out his spout, as much as to say, 'See how that is done'. I have never seen whales at play before or since. It seemed too bad to interrupt their pastime, but they were the fish we had crossed three oceans into the fourth to find.

Heavy dark clouds and flying mist enclosed the ship so that nothing two or three miles away in any direction could be seen from her. Still, when the captain gave the order, 'Line in three larboard boats!' every man sprung to his station as though the sea was calm and the wind was light.

'Hoist and swing! Lower away.'

Down went the three boats on the lee side, which was the larboard. It required quick and experienced movements to get the boats away from the ship's side without swamping or having them stoven.

'Use great caution', was the last word to us as we shoved off. The captain sprang on top of the tryworks to observe our movements. As much could be seen from there as from aloft, the storm clouds were so close around us.

Our boat succeeded in getting out oars and pulling first. It was no fit time to hoist sails, and when we crossed the ship's bows the other boats were two or three ship's lengths astern of us. So, if the whales did not go down, our chance to be amongst them first was good.

After pulling before the wind and sea a short time, I looked over my shoulder ahead of the boat, and as the boat rose I could see the whales tumbling and rolling no great distance

off. By the way we were shooting over the water, not many minutes more would elapse before I should have passed through my trial, and be honoured, or disgraced, as a boat-steerer; and, if failing, I would be disrated, sent forward, and never more have a chance to become above the common sailor on board a whale ship. These thoughts went through my mind, and although I did not fear a whale it made me nervous, as this would be the first time for me to strike one. The captain was plainly to be seen on top of the tryworks with his spyglass, watching our boat as she approached the whales.

As we got on the top of a big sea, the second mate sternly sang out to me:

'Stand up!'

Peaking my oar, jumping to my feet, grasping the first iron in my hands, mind made up to do or die, I saw three whales right ahead. I was looking down at them as they lay in the hollow of the sea, and could make out every part of their upper sides and plainly see their big flukes in motion as they slowly twisted them from side to side. They, like us, were heading to the leeward, and perfectly unaware of the sharp cruel iron that would soon penetrate one of their sides. I had hardly time to brace myself firmly against the clumsy cleat when the boat shot down the side of the sea, and amid the roar of breaking water with the boat's head a few feet clear of the whale, I darted first one iron and then the other chock to the hitches, just forward his hump.

Never in my life have I had such feelings of relief and pleasure, as I saw the line run out when the whale dove into the depths, drawing it after him.

The captain (so I was told afterwards by the boat-steerer of the fourth mate's boat, which did not lower) had his glass on us just before we struck, and when I stood up he was all excitement, saying, 'He stand up! Only strike that whale and I will give you anything I have, anything except my wife'; and as my irons struck the whale he threw off his hat, saying, 'He is fast! Take my wife and all I have!'

I guess he forgot about his offers after we got on board, for I got nothing but the proud satisfaction that I had struck my first whale and proved that a boy only seventeen years old could fill a man's place on a whaleman's deck.

The Narrative of a Voyage by Nelson Cole Haley, Harpooner in the ship Charles W. Morgan 1849–1853

The Battle of the Summer Islands

A lasting noise, as horrid and as loud
As thunder makes before it breaks the cloud.
Three days they dread this murmur, ere they know
From what blind cause th'unwonted sound may grow.
At length two monsters of unequal size,
Hard by the shore, a fisherman espies;
Two mighty whales! which swelling seas had toss'd,
And left them pris'ners on the rocky coast.
One as a mountain vast, and with her came
A cub, not much inferior to his dam.
Here in a pool, among the rocks engaged,
They roar'd like lions caught in toils, and raged.
The man knew what they were, who heretofore
Had seen the like lie murder'd on the shore;
By the wild fury of some tempest cast,
The fate of ships, and shipwreck'd men, to taste.
As careless dames, whom wine and sleep betray
To frantic dreams, their infants overlay:
So there, sometimes, the raging ocean fails,
And her own brood exposes; when the whales
Against sharp rocks, like reeling vessels quash'd,
Though huge as mountains, are in pieces dash'd;

Along the shore their dreadful limbs lie scatter'd,
Like hills with earthquakes shaken, torn, and
shatter'd.

…

The bigger whale like some huge carrack lay,
Which wanteth sea-room with her foes to play;
Slowly she swims; and when, provoked, she would
Advance her tail, her head salutes the mud;
The shallow water doth her force infringe,
And renders vain her tail's impetuous swinge;
The shining steel her tender sides receive,
And there, like bees, they all their weapons leave.

…

Blood flows in rivers from her wounded side,
As if they would prevent the tardy tide,
And raise the flood to that propitious height,
As might convey her from this fatal strait.
She swims in blood, and blood does spouting throw
To heaven, that heaven men's cruelties might know.
Their fixed jav'lins in her side she wears,
And on her back a grove of pikes appears;
You would have thought, had you the monster seen
Thus dress'd, she had another island been:
Roaring she tears the air with such a noise,
As well resembled the conspiring voice
Of routed armies, when the field is won,
To reach the ears of her escaped son.
He, though a league removed from the foe,
Hastes to her aid; the pious Trojan so,

The Battle of the Summer Islands

The right
killers the
blow, hot wi
And they r

Neglecting for Creusa's life his own,

Repeats the danger of the burning town.

The men, amazed, blush to see the seed

Of monsters human piety exceed.

Well proves this kindness, what the Grecian sung,

That love's bright mother from the ocean sprung.

Their courage droops, and hopeless now, they wish

For composition with th'unconquered fish;

So she their weapons would restore again,

Through rocks they'd hew her passage to the main.

But how instructed in each other's mind?

Or what commerce can men with monsters find?

Not daring to approach their wounded foe,

Whom her courageous son protected so,

They charge their muskets, and, with hot desire

Of fell revenge, renew the fight with fire;

Standing aloof, with lead they bruise the scales,

And tear the flesh of the incensed whales.

But no success their fierce endeavours found,

Nor this way could they give one fatal wound.

Now to their fort they are about to send

For the loud engines which their isle defend;

But what those pieces framed to batter walls,

Would have effected on those mighty whales,

Great Neptune will not have us know, who sends

A tide so high that it relieves his friends.

And thus they parted with exchange of harms;

Much blood the monsters lost, and they their arms.

Edmund Waller, *The Battle of the Summer Islands*, 1645

The Battle of the Summer Islands

The right
killers there
blow, hot wild
And they roa

Fortunat's Abentheuer zu Wasser und zu Lande.
Zauberspiel von Lembert.

Fortunat: Was schickt uns den unser neuer Hausherr heut zum Frühstück - Peter: Ganz frische Häring, ich bin g'rad im Magen g'essen
weis unser Hausherr verschlungen hat.

CAPTAIN PADDOCK'S WHALE IRON

One of the most singular incidents in connection with the exploits of Nantucket's whalemen and whaleships was that of Peter Paddock. Captain Paddock struck a whale in the Pacific ocean and 'lost his iron', the whale escaping. Thirteen years later, while on another voyage in the Pacific, he struck a whale and when it was being cut up, the iron which he lost so many years previous was found imbedded in the flesh. It bore his own initials 'P. P.', and was easily identified as the lost iron. That Captain Paddock should strike the same whale after a lapse of thirteen years and thus recover his iron himself was considered most remarkable by the Nantucket whalemen.

The Nantucket Scrap Basket, 1916

Six miles of whale line

The quantity of line withdrawn from the different boats engaged in the capture was singularly great. It amounted altogether, to 10,400 yards, or nearly six English miles. Of these, thirteen new lines were lost, together with the sunken boat, the harpoon connecting them to the fish having dropt out before the whale was killed.

John D. Goodman, *American Natural History*, 1828

An aquatic
BATTLE SCENE

The scene of slaughter was exceedingly picturesque and unusually
exciting, especially on a calm morning, when the mirage would transform
not only the boats and their crews into fantastic imagery, but the whales,
as they sent forth their towering spouts of aqueous vapor, frequently
tinted with blood, would appear greatly distorted ... The boats ... would
be seen gliding over the molten-looking surface of the water, with a ...
colossal form of the whale appearing for an instant, like a spectre ... while
the report of the bomb-guns would sound like the sudden discharge of
musketry; but one cannot fully realise, unless he be an eyewitness, the
intense and boisterous excitement of the reckless pursuit ... Numbers of
[boats] will be fast to whales at the same time, and the stricken animals,
in their efforts to escape, can be seen darting in every direction through
the water, or breaching headlong clear of its surface, coming down with a
splash that sends columns of foam in every direction ... The men in the
boats shout and yell ... it is one continually changing aquatic battle scene.

Captain Charles Scammon, 1857

The whale's *flurry*

The whales killed at the Portland fishery were of two kinds, the right or black whale, and the sperm whale. The right whale has an immense tongue, and lives by suction, the food being a kind of small shrimp. When in a flurry — that is, when she has received her death-stroke with the lance — she goes round in a circle, working with her head and flukes. The sperm whales feed on squid, which they bite, and when in a flurry they work with the head and flukes, and with the mouth open, and often crush the boats.

George Dunderdale, *The Book of the Bush*, 1898

Awaite Pawana!

As soon as they arrive in those latitudes where they expect to meet
with whales, a man is sent up to the mast-head; if he sees one, he
immediately cries out AWAITE PAWANA, here is a whale; they all
remain still and silent until he repeats PAWANA, a whale, when in
less than six minutes the two boats are launched, filled with every
implement necessary for the attack.

J. Hector St John de Crevecoeur, *Letters from an American Farmer*, 1782

SLAUGHTER OF THE BEAST

Imperceptibly we slackened speed until we tailed the big cow about thirty yards ahead.
The ponderous plunging of the slow-moving whale seemed to be the most dominant
sound. On deck, even though the majority of our crew were by this time well seasoned
to the game, there was an atmosphere of tension and impending drama. Every face,
except the helmsman's, was transfixed on the intended victim. Every action on board
was now directed towards the slaughter of the beast ahead of us.

Peter Lancaster Brown, *Coast of Coral and Pearl*, 1972

A flash and a splash

Quick as thought ... thunders the Greener's gun, while the whaleline tears over the boat's gunwale. A flash, a splash, and a hole in the water tells where the whale had been. For a second, all is quiet, as the hurt Leviathan, with its deadly harpoon deep in his flesh behind the left flipper, sulks at the bottom of the bay. Scant time has the crew for a hasty 'hurrah' and wave of the caps, when, stung by the rankly barb, the alarmed monster tears away, towing the boat behind him at more than race-horse speed. East, west, north, and south he dashes in mad endeavor to free himself from the harmful harpoon and its ominous attachments.

Edward Berwick, 'Offshore Whaling in The Bay of Monterey', *The Cosmopolitan*, 1900

HIGH TIDE *in Boston*

Charlestown likewise suffer'd very much; and we hear a great number of Whaleboats have been carry'd from the shore towards Cape Codd, where the Tide was never known to come before.

Benjamin Franklin, 'High Tide in Boston', *The New-England Courant*, 4 March 1722/3

A DYING WHALE

The muscles and tissues were still alive, practically as full of life as they had been a minute before when the creature was, if not a thing of beauty in appearance, a marvellous living mechanism. She was now like a wound-up clock with nothing to put the pendulum in motion, a vast mass of living cells still ready to do their duty, but with the central nervous system shot away and the amazing telegraphic system of nerves completely out of gear. Some tissues were still doing their job. Here and there a muscle quivered and twitched. She was a hulk of dead and living tissues, each cell craving for the oxygen and food supplies which were being denied it. A little longer and the great beast would be a dead mass, a thing of value only in terms of industrial processes; workmen in the chemical factories of far-off lands would earn wages by treating the fatty compounds, the products of its former living activities.

❧

It is always after the excitement is over that regret and depression come, and I think it would be impossible for even a seasick landholder to miss the thrill whilst a whale hunt is on. But one later has other feelings. No one who has seen a whale die can ever think of it unconcernedly as a fish.

William Dakin, 1915

DEEPLY DYED WITH BLOOD

The seamen now seized the whale-line, and slowly drew their boat to within a few feet of the tail of the fish, whose progress became sensibly less rapid, as he grew weak with the loss of blood. In a few minutes he stopped running, and appeared to roll uneasily on the water, as if suffering the agony of death.

'Shall we pull in, and finish him, Tom?' cried Barnstable; 'a few sets from your bayonet would do it'.

The cockswain stood examining his game, with cool discretion, and replied to this interrogatory —

'No, sir, no — he's going into his flurry; there's no occasion for disgracing ourselves by using a soldier's weapon in taking a whale. Starn off, sir, starn off! The creater's in his flurry!'

The warning of the prudent cockswain was promptly obeyed, and the boat cautiously drew off to a distance, leaving to the animal a clear space, while under its dying agonies. From a state of perfect rest, the terrible monster threw its tail on high, as when in sport, but its blows were trebled in rapidity and violence, till all was hid from view by a pyramid of foam, that was deeply dyed with blood. The roarings of the fish were like the bellowings of a herd of bulls, and to one who was ignorant of the fact, it would have appeared as if a thousand monsters were engaged in deadly combat, behind the bloody mist that obstructed the view. Gradually, these effects subsided, and when the discoloured water again settled down to the long and regular swell of the ocean, the fish was seen, exhausted, and yielding passively to its fate. As life departed, the enormous black mass rolled to one side, and when the white and glistening skin of the belly became apparent, the seamen well knew that their victory was achieved.

James Fenimore Cooper, *The Pilot*, 1806

Belly Up and dead

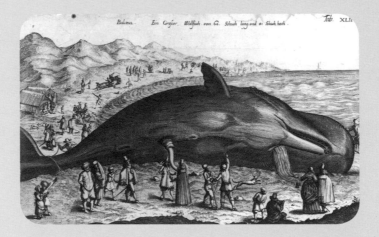

Not ten minutes after this, the first mate, who had gone aloft into the crow's-nest to take a look-out round, eagerly shouted, 'A fish! a fish! See, she spouts!' and down on deck he hurried with all despatch …

Away they pulled. I looked over the side, and saw the whale a mile off, floating, thoughtless of danger, on the surface of the ocean, and spouting out a fountain of water high into the air. I fancied that I could even hear the deep 'roust' she made as she respired the air, without which she cannot exist any more than animals of the land or air. Every one on deck follows the boats with eager eyes. The boat makes a circuit, so as to approach the monster in the rear; for if he sees them, he will be off far down into the ocean, and may not rise for a long distance away. With rapid strokes they pull on, but as noiselessly as possible. The headmost boat is within ten fathoms of the fish — I am sure it will be ours. The harpooner stands up in the bows with harpoon in hand. Suddenly, with tail in air, down dives the monster; and the faces of all around me assume an expression of black disappointment. It must be remembered that, as all on board benefit by every fish which is caught, all are interested in the capture of one.

'It's a loose fall, after all', said old David, who was near me. 'I thought so. I shouldn't be surprised if we went home with a clean ship after all.' …

On they pull. Then on a sudden appears the mighty monster. She has risen to the surface to breathe, a 'fair start' from the boat. The harpooner stands up, with his unerring weapon in his hand: when was it ever known to miss its aim? The new-fangled gun he disdains. A few strong and steady strokes, and the boat is close to the whale. The harpoon is launched from his hank, and sinks deep into the oily flesh.

The boat is enveloped in a cloud of spray — the whole sea around is one mass of foam. Has the monster struck her, and hurled her gallant crew to destruction? No; drawn rapidly along, her broad bow ploughing up the sea, the boat is seen to emerge from the mist with a jack flying as a signal that she is fast, while the mighty fish is diving far below it, in a vain effort to escape.

Now arose from the mouth of every seaman on deck the joyful cry of 'A fall, a fall!' at the same time that every one jumped and stamped on deck, to arouse the sleepers below to hasten to the assistance of their comrades. We all then rushed to the boat-falls.

Never, apparently, were a set of men in such a desperate hurry. Had the ship been sinking, or even about to blow up, we could scarcely have made more haste.

The falls were let go, and the boats in the water, as the watch below rushed on deck. Many of the people were dressed only in their drawers, stockings, and shirts, while the rest of their clothes were in their hands, fastened together by a lanyard; but without stopping to put them on, they tumbled into the boats, and seized their oars ready to shove off …

'Hurra, boys! see, she rises!' was the general shout. Up came the whale, more suddenly than we expected. A general dash was made at her by all the boats. 'Stern for your lives; stern of all!' cried some of the more experienced harpooners. 'See, she's in a flurry.'

First the monster flapped the water violently with its fins; then its tail was elevated aloft, lashing the ocean around into a mass of foam. This was not its death-flurry; for, gaining strength before any more harpoons or lances could be struck into it, away it went again, heading towards the ice. Its course was now clearly discerned by a small whirling eddy, which showed that it was at no great distance under the surface, while in its wake was seen a thin line of oil and blood, which had exuded from its wound.

Wearied, however, by its exertions and its former deep dive, it was again obliged to come to the surface to breathe. Again the eager boats dashed in, almost running on its back, and from every side it was plied with lances, while another harpoon was driven deeply into it, to make it doubly secure. Our boat was the most incautious, for we were right over the tail of the whale. The chief harpooner warned us — 'Back, my lads; back of all', he shouted out, his own boat pulling away. 'Now she's in her death-flurry truly.'

The words were not out of his mouth when I saw our harpooner leap from the boat, and swim as fast as he could towards one of the others. I was thinking of following his example, knowing he had good reasons for it, for I had seen the fins of the animal flap furiously, and which had warned him, when a violent blow, which I fancied must have not only dashed the boat to pieces, but have broken every bone in our bodies, was struck on the keel of the boat.

Up flew the boat in the air, some six or eight feet at least, with the remaining crew in her. Then down we came, one flying on one side, one on the other, but none of us hurt even, all spluttering and striking out together; while the boat came down keel uppermost, not much the worse either. Fortunately we all got clear of the furious blows the monster continued dealing with its tail.

'Never saw a whale in such a flurry', said old David, into whose boat I was taken. For upwards of two minutes the flurry continued, we all the while looking on, and no one daring to approach it; at the same time a spout of blood and mucus and oil ascended into the air from its blow-holes, and sprinkled us all over.

'Hurra, my lads, she spouts blood!' we shouted out to each other, though we all saw and felt it plain enough. There was a last lash of that tail, now faint and scarce rising above the water, but which, a few minutes ago, would have sent every boat round it flying into splinters. Then all was quiet. The mighty mass, now almost inanimate, turned slowly round upon its side, and then it floated belly up and dead.

W. H. G. Kingston, *Peter the Whaler*, 1851

A Rousing Whaling Song

A MIGHTY WHALE WE RUSH UPON,
AND IN OUR IRONS THROW:
SHE SINKS HER MONSTROUS BODY DOWN
AMONG THE WAVES BELOW.

AND WHEN SHE RISES OUT AGAIN,
WE SOON RENEW THE FIGHT;
THRUST OUR SHARP LANCES IN AMAIN,
AND ALL HER RAGE EXCITE.

ENRAGED, SHE MAKES A MIGHTY BOUND;
THICK FOAMS THE WHITENED SEA;
THE WAVES IN CIRCLES RISE AROUND,
AND WIDENING ROLL AWAY.

SHE THRASHES WITH HER TAIL AROUND,
AND BLOWS HER REDDENING BREATH;
SHE BREAKS THE AIR, A DEAFENING SOUND,
WHILE OCEAN GROANS BENEATH.

FROM NUMEROUS WOUNDS, WITH CRIMSON FLOOD,
SHE STAINS THE FROTHY SEAS,
AND GASPS, AND BLOWS HER LATEST BLOOD,
WHILE QUIVERING LIFE DECAYS.

John Osborn, 'A Rousing Whaling Song', c.1750

CUTTING IN THE WHALE

When we commenced to cut in our whale next morning, the sea was fairly alive with fish of innumerable kinds, while a vast host of sea-birds, as usual, waited impatiently for the breaking-up of the huge carcass, which they knew would afford them no end of a feast. An untoward accident, which happened soon after the work was started, gave the waiting myriads immense satisfaction, although the unfortunate second mate, whose slip of the spade was responsible, came in for a hurricane of vituperation from the enraged skipper. It was in detaching the case from the head — always a work of difficulty, and requiring great precision of aim. Just as Mr. Cruce made a powerful thrust with his keen tool, the vessel rolled, and the blow, missing the score in which he was cutting, fell upon the case instead, piercing its side. For a few minutes the result was unnoticed amidst the wash of the ragged edges of the cut, but presently a long streak of white, wax-like pieces floating astern, and a tremendous commotion among the birds, told the story. The liquid spermaceti was leaking rapidly from the case, turning solid as it got into the cool water. Nothing could be done to stop the waste, which, as it was a large whale, was not less than twenty barrels, or about two tuns of pure spermaceti.

Frank T. Bullen, *The Cruise of the 'Cachalot'*, 1898

The Whale is harpooned to be sure; but bethink you, how you would manage a powerful unbroken colt, with the mere appliance of a rope tied to the root of his tail.

W. A. G., *Ribs and Trucks from Davy's Locker*, 1842

GULATHING LAW *11th century Norse*

A hauld or a man of higher rank, [if he comes upon a whale that is no more than] eighteen ells in length, has the right to the entire whale; any other man [has the right] to one half as long. If a man comes upon a whale, he shall cut it up before witnesses, or let him leave the backbone, the head, and the tail fin; then these parts, if he has no witnesses, shall testify for him. He shall cut it up in the water and shall not carry [the parts] up on the green sod; if he does bring them up, the owner of the land shall have one-half of the whale, unless he [the finder] shall redeem it with the fine for trespass, thinking the whale of greater worth. If a man proceeds to cut up a whale where the grass is sufficient to feed a ewe and a lamb in the summer, he shall redeem the parts with the fine for trespass if he brings them up [on the land].

Can he who has discovered only some of the values of whalebone and whale oil be said to have discovered the true use of the whale?

Henry David Thoreau, *Journal*, 1853

WITCHES BREW

In less time than it will take you to read this, of course, the whale was nearly out of sight. As he moved away majestically, a quatrain from Moby Dick came into my mind — one from the introductory pages which Herman Melville credits to an hypothetical 'sub-sub-librarian'. I began to sing it, not knowing whether or not it ever had a tune, and devised the following, which might go well if arranged for a quartet of lusty young throats. What think ye, Grace and Captain Ahab, of a song by Melville and Murphy?

> Oh the rare old Whale, mid storm and gale
> In his ocean home will be
> A giant in might, where might is right,
> And King of the boundless sea.

October 2. Evidently we are once more on sperm whale grounds. At half past six this morning the boats were down after a big bull, but again in vain. In midmorning, however, a school was sighted and the lowering, hauling aback, and all other maneuvers were repeated.

The three boats became widely scattered, and one went so far out into the dim horizon that we lost sight of it for a time. However, each crew killed its whale. It was half past three in the afternoon before we had the carcasses all alongside, and also before anybody had a dollop of grub beyond his early breakfast. Moreover, the meal was a quick and poor one, and Mr. da Lomba got the cutting-in started without stopping for a bite.

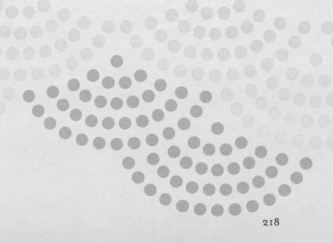

All three whales were rather small, and the cutting-in was completed at night. Then mincing and boiling were begun, while the last whale was still being hacked and stripped by artificial illumination. Between half past eight and nine o'clock in the evening we had supper in shifts. The meal was at least hearty — hash of salt beef, potatoes and onions, sperm whale steak, corn hoecakes and tea. Work is to be continued through the night.

October 3. I stayed up until all hours, watching every process, moving about the dusky, slippery deck, or sitting atop the cabin, in a whaleboat on the davits, or anywhere else that offered a good view. If there is any modern counterpart of an uncouth revel around a witches' brew, it is the scene of the trypots at night.

It was eight bells (midnight) when we had cut-in the final fish. The *Daisy*, with topsails aback, rolled gently in the quiet swell, while the officers on the cutting stage punched with their spades as best they could in the dismal light of lanterns and oil-soaked torches. The flickering glare showed the hulk of the whale alongside the flash of bloody wavelets beyond. On deck a cresset, or bug light, of burning blubber scrap, and the fiery chimneys of the tryworks in full blast, cast enough illumination to reveal the great blankets of blubber and the greasy, toiling figures scurrying about amid the shouting of orders, the creak of tackles and the clank of chains. At six bells the last strip came over the plank-sheer. The severed head of the whale floated by the starboard quarter, lashed securely and ready to be handled at day-break. Only the rite of the whaleman's ultimate hope remained to be carried out before the flensed carcass should be cut adrift.

Robert Cushman, *Logbook for Grace: Whaling Brig Daisy*, 1912–1913

漁夫解剖圖

Living in a whale

Nature has taken thought for the inhabitants and enabled them to construct houses and all the requisite furniture within the gigantic ribs of these animals … it is a known fact that the bones which remain are so strong and enormous that people can produce from them entire homes: walls, doors, windows, roofs, chairs, and even tables. The ribs are twenty to thirty feet long, or even more, while the spinal vertebrae and the forked bones of the colossal skull are themselves of no small magnitude …. Once the flesh and internal organs of the massive beast have wasted away and perished, only the bones remain, in the shape of a huge keel. After the skeleton has eventually been cleansed by rains and fresh air, strong men are enlisted to erect it in the form of a house. The one who is supervising its construction exerts himself to put windows at the top of the building or in the monster's sides, and divides the interior into several comfortable living quarters. The doors are made from the creature's hide, which has long since been stripped off for this or some different purpose and hardened by the rough winds.

Olaus Magnus, *A Description of the Northern Peoples*, 1555

Accept, dear Girl this busk from me, carved by my humble hand.
I took it from a Sparm Whale's Jaw, one thousand miles from land!
In many a gale has been the Whale in which this bone did rest,
His time is past, his bone at last, must now support thy brest.

Scrimshaw engraving

At home *with a whale*

Olaus writes that churches and houses are made from the ribs of whales, and doors from whaleskin.

In the countries where there are many large whales, that is in the Northern countries, the people often use the ribs of whales and other large monsters to make houses and chapels and for household utensils. For if these very big fish are driven on to dry land by the force of other creatures that are their enemies, or are caught and dragged on land by human skill, and then they lie rotten and used up on the sand, or all the meat and train-oil has been used by people, then it is clear that the big bones will not simply be left lying there unused. They can be used to make whole houses, walls, doors, window-frames, roofs, benches and tables. These ribs are 20 or 30 or more feet long. And then there are the pieces of the spinal column and the large split bones of the head, which through the skill of the craftsmen are fitted into one another with files and saws so neatly that a carpenter couldn't do a better job with iron nails. Olaus describes this in his 21st book on the countries of the North.

When there is no more flesh left on the bones and the entrails have been removed, there is not much of these large fish left except the bones, which lie there like big ships that lie upside-down with the hull upwards. After a while they are cleaned by the rain and the air, and then groups of people toil to erect them as houses. Window-frames are made from them in the tops of the roofs or in the side, and they are divided up into many comfortable homes. But the doors are made from the skin of these creatures, which has been removed long before and hardened in the biting wind. Separate stalls are made for pigs and other animals in these houses, just as people do in other kinds of houses. There is always some space left under the roof for the cockerels, which are there instead of clocks to wake people up in the night to go and work, because it is night there the whole winter long. People who sleep beneath these whale ribs often dream that they are in great danger at sea and are at risk of drowning in a storm. This is what Olaus writes.

Adriaen Coenen, *The Whale Book*, 1585

WHALEBONE CORSETS

Moreover, you will always be able to get whalebone, just as you will always be able to get gold and diamonds. But, whatever the scarcity and whatever the price, Redfern Corsets will always be stiffened with whalebone, because there is nothing else fit for a fine corset. No woman who knows the art of dressing will have anything but a whalebone corset. She'd have it if it cost $100.00.

Frank Finney, *A Woman Has an Awful Lot to Thank a Whale for*, 1909

CUTTING UP A WHALE—GATHERING THE SPERMACETI FROM THE HEAD.

t whales, the sperm-whales, the

WHALE OIL CANDLES

Winter Strained Sperm Oil In the fall, or autumn, the oil is boiled for the purpose of granulation during the approaching cold weather. The oil thus passes from a purely liquid into a solid state, or one in which it is in grains, or masses. When the temperature of the atmosphere rises, or the weather slackens during the winter, the oil which has been frozen, but is now somewhat softened, is shoveled out of the casks and put into strong bags that will hold half a bushel or more, in order to be pressed …

    Spring Sperm Oil What remains in the bags after the first pressing, is again heated by being put into boilers, after which it is baled into casks again, and upon cooling, it becomes more compact and solid than it was before. During the month of April, when the temperature is about 50 degrees, the oil becomes softened; it is then put into bags, and goes through a second process of pressing …

    Tight Pressed Oil That which is left in the bags after the second pressing, is again melted, and put into tin pans or tubs which will hold about 40 pounds each. When this liquid is thoroughly cooled, as each pressing makes what is left harder … the cakes taken from the tubs are then carried into a room heated to about 90 degrees; and as they begin to yield to the influence of this high temperature, or the remaining oil begins to soften the cakes, they are taken and shaved into very fine pieces, or ground up in some instances, deposited in bags as hitherto, and put into the hydraulic press … the bags subjected to a powerful pressure of 300 tons or more, all the oil is extracted from them, and what is left is perfectly dry, free from any oily matter, and brittle …

    Spermaceti What remains after the several pressings, and the removal of all the oil, is called stearine, or spermaceti … the spermaceti from the head oil is quite different from that of the body oil; the former presents fine, bright transparent scales like small particles of isinglass, while the later is more compact, something like dough. In cooling, one exhibits a sparry, crystalline structure, the other that of clay. Head oil or matter is usually manufactured with the body oil of the whale, and mixed in proportion to one-third of the former to two-thirds of the latter.

    Spermaceti Candles … The oil, it is supposed, is wholly extracted, and nothing now remains but the spermaceti. Its color, however, is not white, but interspersed with grayish streaks, bordering on the yellow. The spermaceti is put into large boilers adapted for the purpose, and heated to the temperature of 210 degrees. It is refined and cleared of all foreign ingredients by the application of alkali. Afterwards water is added, which, with a temperature of 240 degrees, throws off the alkali in the form of vapor. The liquid which remains is as pure and clear as the crystal water, and ready to be made into the finest spermaceti candles.

Lewis Holmes, The Arctic Whaleman, 1861

CATCHING WHALES

I never shall forget what a long chase I had with a whale once. Shall I tell you about it, little friend? There was a man in the ship who was looking out for whales … Well, all at once, the man who was looking out the day I speak of, when I had such a run, sung out as loud as he could, 'There she blows!' We all knew what that meant. That is what they always say when they see a whale. It means, 'There is a whale come up to breathe.' This whale was a great way off. I should think he was a mile from the ship.

Well, the captain told some of us to get into a boat, and to go out after the whale. We did so … We rowed as fast as we could, until we came up near where the whale was lying.

Oh, what a large whale! As soon as the boat got near enough, one man threw two harpoons at the whale, and they both stuck fast in his flesh …

As soon as the whale felt these irons in his side, he began to run. I never knew before that a whale could swim so fast. It took him only a very little while to run out with all the loose rope; and our boat went through the water pretty fast, you may be sure. I was afraid the whale would take it into his head to dive down towards the bottom. If he had gone down, we should have gone with him, unless we could have cut the rope. But he did not go down. Away we went, as fast as if we had been on a railroad. He was all the time taking us further from the ship. 'Well,' we thought, 'what is going to become of us!' The whale did not seem to care any thing about that. I suppose he thought that was our look-out, and not his.

But the fellow got tired out by and by. He had bled so much, that he began to grow faint. At last he went so slow, that we rowed up to him, and stabbed him with a long knife. He died pretty soon after that, and we got more than two hundred barrels of oil out of him.

Catching whales seems a cruel business to you. It is a cruel business. I never liked it. But somebody must do it. The butcher who kills oxen, and sheep, and calves, has to be cruel. But we must have butchers. We must have people to kill whales, though you never will catch me chasing after a whale again, as long as my name is Jack Mason.

Theodore Thinker, *Jack Mason, the Old Sailor*, 1850

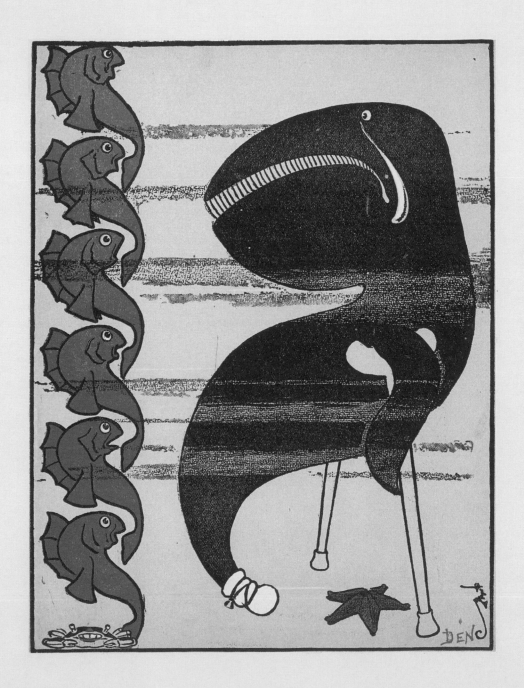

Captain Nemo's
hunting ethics

CAPTAIN NEMO OBSERVED the herd of cetaceans cavorting on the waters a mile from the Nautilus.

'They're southern right whales,' he said. 'There goes the fortune of a whole whaling fleet.'

'Well, sir,' the Canadian asked, 'couldn't I hunt them, just so I don't forget my old harpooning trade?'

'Hunt them? What for?' Captain Nemo replied. 'Simply to destroy them? We have no use for whale oil on this ship.'

'But, sir,' the Canadian went on, 'in the Red Sea you authorized us to chase a dugong!'

'There it was an issue of obtaining fresh meat for my crew. Here it would be killing for the sake of killing. I'm well aware that's a privilege reserved for mankind, but I don't allow such murderous pastimes. When your peers, Mr Land, destroy decent, harmless creatures like the southern right whale or the bowhead whale, they commit a reprehensible offense. Thus they've already depopulated all of Baffin Bay, and they'll wipe out a whole class of useful animals. So leave these poor cetaceans alone. They have quite enough natural enemies, such as sperm whales, swordfish, and sawfish, without you meddling with them.'

I'll let the reader decide what faces the Canadian made during this lecture on hunting ethics. Furnishing such arguments to a professional harpooner was a waste of words. Ned Land stared at Captain Nemo and obviously missed his meaning. But the captain was right. Thanks to the mindless, barbaric bloodthirstiness of fishermen, the last baleen whale will someday disappear from the ocean.

Jules Verne, *Twenty Thousand Leagues Under the Sea*, 1870

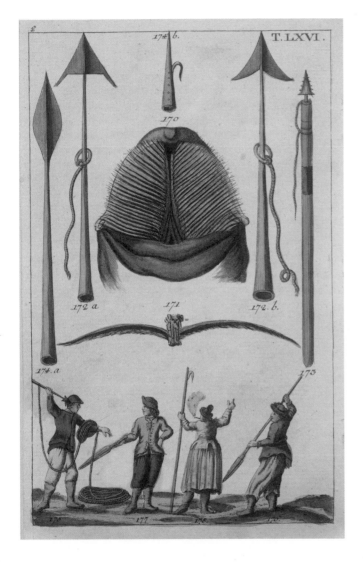

THE POOR WHALE

The idea sometimes advanced by captains of ships, who ought to know better, that 'there are now as many whales as ever there were, that they had only been driven from particular grounds, Ec.' is preposterous in the extreme. A simple calculation will shew the utter fallacy of such an assertion. There were upon the North West and Kamschatka, last season [1844], 300 ships. Each of these struck, and captured, or so badly wounded that they afterwards died, we will say 40 whales, and I knew one to have struck 75 whales in taking a thousand barrels … The poor whale is doomed to utter extermination, or at least, so near to it that too few will remain to tempt the cupidity of man.

M. E. Bowles, 'Some Account of the Whale-Fishery of the N. West Coast and Kamschatka,' *Polynesian,* 4 October 1845

Where are your combing seas, your blue water, your rollers,
your breakers, your whales, or your waterspouts?

James Fenimore Cooper, *The Pathfinder*, 1840

WHERE *went* THAT SPIRIT?

Marble would not be good enough to lay this corpse upon; for the sight —
discard the blemishes — is wonder. This is the sordid remnant, yet the eye may
even now replace what has been lost … Where went that spirit, which played in
the magnificence — which made this mountain leap and sport, quickened the eye,
retracted that balloon of a tongue, lifted that fallen jaw? This was a lump which
solved some wild equation of the elements. This monstrous form and painted
shapeliness has burned its way through phosphorescent waves in summer, the black
night lighted by luminous clouds of its own breathing; and sinking with an easy
silence, it has spiralled to unseen depths, upon unknown desires.

F.V.Morley, *Whaling North and South*, 1926

Now the vast dusk bulk that is the whale's bulk, it seems mine;
Warily, sportsman! though I lie so sleepy and sluggish,
the tap of my flukes is death.

Walt Whitman, 'The Sleepers', 1900

MASTER to Disciple

MASTER: Where do you sell your fish?

FISHERMAN: In the town.

MASTER: Who buys them?

FISHERMAN: The citizens. I cannot catch as much as I can sell.

MASTER: What fish do you take?

FISHERMAN: Herring, salmon, porpoises, sturgeon, oysters, crabs, mussels, periwinkles, cockles, plaice, sole, lobsters, and the like.

MASTER: Do you wish to capture a whale?

FISHERMAN: No.

MASTER: Why?

FISHERMAN: Because it is a dangerous thing to capture a whale. It is safer for me to go to the river with my boat than to go with many ships hunting whales.

MASTER: Why so?

FISHERMAN: Because I prefer to take a fish that I can kill rather than one which with a single blow can sink or kill not only me but also my companions.

MASTER: Yet many people do capture whales and escape the danger, and they obtain a great price for what they do.

FISHERMAN: You speak the truth, but I do not dare because of my cowardice.

The Dialogue Between Master and Disciple: On Laborers, c.1000

The enormous mass

At first sight of the enormous mass, my wife and Frank were quite startled; and no wonder, for I conjectured that the whale could not be less than sixty feet long, and nearly thirty feet in thickness near the head, and in weight it must have exceeded two hundred tons.

The most remarkable thing appeared, however, to be the fact that the head should be one-third the length of the whole body, and the eyes not larger than those of an ox. The interior of the jaw was lined with long, dark, and flexible bones, some of them in the roof of the mouth being at least ten or twelve feet long.

These, I told the boys, were called 'whalebone,' and very useful in many ways, as well as a most valuable article of commerce.

Another circumstance that surprised us all was the size of the tongue, which if removed would have weighed nearly a thousand pounds. The deep abyss of the frightful throat also created great surprise among the boys, and Fritz expressed his wonder that such an enormous monster should have such a small gullet.

And this wonder was natural, for it appeared scarcely large enough to admit my arm ...

Fritz and Jack instantly slipped on the foot-straps, and, mounting on the back of the whale, ran over the monster from the tail to the head. I then desired Fritz to cut off the upper lip with his hatchet, while I separated the lower part from the jaw with my chopper. This exposed the whalebone, and gave me an opportunity to remove from the head nearly a hundred strips. The mother, assisted by Ernest and Frank, then took possession of the whalebone and carried it to the boat, while I and the other boys were exerting our utmost strength in separating from the whale a portion of the skin.

All at once appeared a number of uninvited spectators of our work. The air was filled with carrion birds of all descriptions, while their numbers seemed to increase every minute. They whirled round us in a circle, and at last alighted on the prey with such greediness and boldness, that they positively snatched away the pieces of flesh we had cut off even before our eyes.

W. H. G. Kingston, *The Swiss Family Robinson*, 1879

NO HUMANE WAY TO KILL A WHALE

When I went to school in Albany in the 1970s whale-killing was a brutal fact of life. The sight of whales being butchered onshore was a bizarre tourist attraction. In the almost thirty years since the industry's demise, Australians' attitude toward the marine environment has changed enormously and nowhere else is this social evolution more marked than in our appreciation of cetaceans.

Nowadays whales and dolphins retain a commercial value as live tourist attractions. They grace almost every tourism poster and pamphlet and website, becoming an alternate coat of arms to WA in particular, along with the whaleshark. They are the basis of a sustainable industry — eco-tourism — whose contribution to our economy is considerable. They help keep small coastal communities alive — even towns like Albany, that once thrived on their slaughter.

Beyond economics, though, whales have accrued an even greater worth, something less tangible than a dollar figure. Their cultural value might be much harder to quantify, but anyone who under-estimates it does so at their own peril. In thirty years whales have become emblematic. Ordinary Western Australians are passionate about whales.

For many coastal Western Australians the annual migration of humpbacks and southern right whales helps define the passing of seasons. The glimpses we snatch of them spouting and leaping and resting in bays and coves have become a kind of reassurance, for the more urbanised we become the more we treasure enduring instances of wildness. And the more educated we become about ecology (even if our learning reveals how little we really know) the more seriously we take our mega-fauna. You might say that whales in particular have taught us a little humility in this regard.

When so many marine species and habitats are in serious trouble, the slow recovery of the humpback from the very brink of extinction has given us hope. The fact that they still exist has come to stand as a signal of our own cultural evolution, because we know that if we had not changed our attitudes to whaling a generation ago, and if the majority of nations had not changed alongside us, then there would be as little to see out there on the water as there was when I was a boy, when the only whales you'd glimpse were being sawn up and boiled. If we hadn't progressed in our thinking since the 1970s, there'd likely be no passing whales at all. No whaling industry. No whale-watching. No whales, full stop.

On a recent trip to the Albany region I saw more live whales in a week than I ever saw in all my high school years living, diving and surfing there. This time I wasn't even looking for them; they were visually and ambiently unavoidable, and I can't tell you how good it felt. At a grim time in history it renewed my awe of these great creatures' resilience, but it also restored my faith in the nobler side of human nature.

But nearly three decades on from the cessation of whaling in our waters, it's a shock to realize that humpbacks are not secure in our southern or western waters. Most of us have assumed that this is a battle that has been fought and won. But the price of victory, it seems, is indeed, eternal vigilance. While most nations have moved on, a few have not. Some have been steadily regrouping and retooling for commercial slaughter.

Australian governments and NGOs have been at the forefront of this necessary vigilance. Many diplomatic efforts have been made to bring recalcitrant whalers into the fold. Politicians, public servants and activists have done a lot of good work in good faith. But with limited results. Despite a welter of procedure and process and protocol, whaling activity has increased.

In the effort to curtail this renewed slaughter it seems that two crucial avenues have not been fully investigated. Legal action, and direct action. Given the political and cultural sensitivities involved, neither of these is anybody's idea of the first and best way to solve the problem, but after the failure of all diplomatic and procedural efforts, there seems to be no alternative left.

There is still no humane way to kill a whale.

There is still no sustainable model for a humane whaling industry.

Whaling belongs to an era when issues of sustainability and humane methods had no meaning. That era has passed and it will not be mourned.   Tim Winton, 2007

A POLAR WHALE'S APPEAL

After the first two hunting seasons in the Arctic, The Friend left off its sermonizing long enough to publish a lengthy letter received from the Anadir Sea. Under the date of 'The second Year of Trouble,' it is the only known communiqué from the newly discovered leviathan:

MR. EDITOR, — In behalf of my species, allow an inhabitant of this sea, to make an appeal through your columns to the friends of the whale in general. A few of the knowing old inhabitants of this sea have recently held a meeting to consult respecting our safety, and in some way or other, if possible, to avert the doom that seems to await all of the whale Genus throughout the world, including the Sperm, Right, and Polar whales. Although our situation, and that of our neighbors in the Arctic, is remote from our enemy's country, yet we have been knowing to the progress of affairs in the Japan and Ochotsk seas, the Atlantic and Indian oceans, and all the other 'whaling grounds.' We have imagined that we were safe in these cold regions; but no; within these last two years a furious attack has been made upon us, an attack more deadly and bloody, than any of our race ever experienced in any part of the world. I scorn to speak of the cruelty that has been practised by our blood-thirsty enemies, armed with harpoon and lance; no age or sex has been spared. Multitudes of our species (the Polar), have been murdered in 'cold' blood. Our enemies have wondered at our mild and inoffensive conduct; we have heard them cry, 'there she blows,' and our hearts have quailed as we saw their glittering steel reflecting the sun beams, and realized that in a few moments our life-blood oozing out, would discolor the briny deep in which we have gambolled for scores of years. We have never been trained to contend with a race of warriors, who sail in large three-masted vessels, on the sterns of which we have read 'New Bedford,' 'Sag Harbor,' and 'New London.' … We have heard of the desperate encounters between these whale-killing monsters and our brethren the Right whales on the North-west coast. Some from that quarter have taken shelter in the quiet bays of our sea, others of the spermaciti species from Japan, have also visited us and reported their battles and disasters; they have told us it is no use to contend with the Nortons, the Tabers, the Coffins, the Coxs, the Smiths, the Halseys, and the other families of whale-killers. We Polar whales are a quiet inoffensive race, desirous of life and peace, but, alas, we fear our doom is sealed; we have heard the threat that in one season more we shall all be 'cut up,' and 'tried out.' Is there no redress? I write in behalf of my butchered and dying species. I appeal to the friends of the whole race of whales. Must we all be murdered in cold blood? Must our race become extinct? Will no friends and allies arise and revenge our wrongs? Will our foes be allowed to prey upon us another year? We have heard of the power of the 'Press;' pray give these few lines a place in your columns, and let them go forth to the world. I am known among our enemies as the 'Bow-head,' but I belong to the Old Greenland family.

Yours till death, POLAR WHALE 170

'A Polar Whale's Appeal', *The Friend*, 15 October 1850

Chapter **5**

IN **LEVIATHAN'S** *wake*

The Unconquerable whale

The whale isn't always caught by its pursuers; sometimes it gets away, and often the hunter is the one to come off worst. This is largely due to the immense size difference between human and whale — as one sailor noted, a whale-boat tackling a whale is 'like a tin can on a dog's tail'. The whale is in reality a gentle giant and simply does what it needs to do to escape or scare off its hunter, through instincts of self-preservation or parental concern (as noted in Louis de Rougemont's story of a female whale protecting its young calf). However, through the centuries the whale has often been seen as a terrifying aggressor or even a deceitful and cunning killer. But the most famous cetacean opponent has to be the white whale in *Moby Dick*. In 1820, the whaling vessel *Essex*, which had sailed from Nantucket in 1819, was attacked and sunk by an enormous whale at the equator. This real-life event captured the imagination of Herman Melville who later used it as the basis for his own whale tale. In a fitting end to *Moby Dick,* just as the whale is finally harpooned, the vengeful Captain Ahab is caught in the whale-line and dragged beneath the ocean, following the whale to his death.

… and knowing that after intrepid assaults, the white whale has escaped alive; it cannot be much matter of surprise that some men go further in their superstitions; declaring Moby Dick not only ubiquitous, but immortal.

Herman Melville, *Moby Dick*, 1851

PAQUEBOT ATTAQUÉ PAR UN TROUPEAU DE BALEINES

MOBY DICK
escapes

'There she breaches! there she breaches!' was the cry, as in his immeasurable bravadoes the White Whale tossed himself salmon-like to Heaven. So suddenly seen in the blue plain of the sea, and relieved against the still bluer margin of the sky, the spray that he raised, for the moment, intolerably glittered and glared like a glacier; and stood there gradually fading and fading away from its first sparkling intensity, to the dim mistiness of an advancing shower in a vale.

'Aye, breach your last to the sun, Moby Dick!' cried Ahab, 'thy hour and thy harpoon are at hand! — Down! down all of ye, but one man at the fore. The boats! — stand by!'

Unmindful of the tedious rope-ladders of the shrouds, the men, like shooting stars, slid to the deck, by the isolated backstays and halyards; while Ahab, less dartingly, but still rapidly was dropped from his perch.

'Lower away', he cried, so soon as he had reached his boat — a spare one, rigged the afternoon previous. 'Mr. Starbuck, the ship is thine — away from the boats, but keep near them. Lower, all!'

As if to strike a quick terror into them, by this time being the first assailant himself, Moby Dick had turned, and was now coming for the three crews. Ahab's boat was central; and cheering his men, he told them he would take the whale head-and-head, — that is, pull straight up to his forehead, — a not uncommon thing; for when within a certain limit, such a course excludes the coming onset from the whale's sidelong vision. But ere that close limit was gained, and while yet all three boats were plain as the ship's three masts to his eye; the White Whale churning himself into furious speed, almost in an instant as it were, rushing among the boats with open jaws, and a lashing tail, offered appalling battle on every side; and heedless of the iron darted at him from every boat, seemed only intent on annihilating each separate plank of which those boats were made. But skilfully manoeuvred, incessantly wheeling like trained chargers in the field; the boats for a while eluded him; though, at times, but by a plank's breadth; while all the time, Ahab's unearthly slogan tore every other cry but his to shreds.

But at last in his untraceable evolutions, the White Whale so crossed and recrossed, and in a thousand ways entangled the slack of the three lines now fast to him, that they foreshortened, and, of themselves, warped the devoted boats towards the planted irons in him; though now for a moment the whale drew aside a little, as if to rally for a more tremendous charge. Seizing that opportunity, Ahab first paid out more line; and then was rapidly hauling and jerking in upon it again — hoping that way to disencumber it of some snarls — when lo! — a sight more savage than the embattled teeth of sharks!

Caught and twisted — corkscrewed in the mazes of the line, loose harpoons and lances, with all their bristling barbs and points, came flashing and dripping up to the chocks in the bows of Ahab's boat. Only one thing could be done. Seizing the boat-knife, he critically reached within — through — and then, without — the rays of steel; dragged in the line beyond, passed it, inboard, to the bowsman, and then, twice sundering the rope near the chocks — dropped the intercepted fagot of steel into the sea; and was all fast again. That instant, the White Whale made a sudden rush among the remaining tangles of the other lines; by so doing, irresistibly dragged the more involved boats of Stubb and Flask towards his flukes; dashed them together like two rolling husks on a surf-beaten beach, and then, diving down into the sea, disappeared in a boiling maelstrom, in which, for a space, the odorous cedar chips of the wrecks danced round and round, like the grated nutmeg in a swiftly stirred bowl of punch.

While the two crews were yet circling in the waters, reaching out after the revolving line-tubs, oars, and other floating furniture, while aslope little Flask bobbed up and down like an empty vial, twitching his legs upwards to escape the dreaded jaws of sharks; and Stubb was lustily singing out for some one to ladle him up; and while the old man's line — now parting — admitted of his pulling into the creamy pool to rescue whom he could; — in that wild simultaneousness of a thousand concreted perils, — Ahab's yet unstricken boat seemed drawn up towards Heaven by invisible wires, — as, arrow-like, shooting perpendicularly from the sea, the White Whale dashed his broad forehead against its bottom, and sent it turning over and over, into the air; till it fell again — gunwale down — and Ahab and his men struggled out from under it, like seals from a sea-side cave.

The first uprising momentum of the whale — modifying its direction as he struck the surface — involuntarily launched him along it, to a little distance from the centre of the destruction he had made; and with his back to it, he now lay for a moment slowly feeling with his flukes from side to side; and whenever a stray oar, bit of plank, the least chip or crumb of the boats touched his skin, his tail swiftly drew back, and came sideways smiting the sea. But soon, as if satisfied that his work for that time was done, he pushed his pleated forehead through the ocean, and trailing after him the intertangled lines, continued his leeward way at a traveller's methodic pace.

Herman Melville, *Moby Dick*, 1851

A TIN CAN ON A DOG'S TAIL

In the middle of this fight into which I was putting all I had, I confess to a certain sympathy with the enemy. It seemed reasonable at least that after being pricked with the harpoon that still galled him, and pierced through with the horrible lance, the whale should wish to steer clear of us. This, however, was not at all the mate's idea of a good form and fair play. Standing like an armed crusader in the bow of the boat, Long John da Lomba would scratch his head after the whale had sounded, and mutter, 'I cain't understan' what make that animile so goddam shy!'

Our status, I thought from time to time, was that of the tin can on a dog's tail. We annoyed the whale, but were otherwise pretty helpless.

Robert Cushman, *Logbook for Grace: Whaling Brig Daisy*, 1912–13

In the JAWS OF THE WHALE
Narrative of the Travels and Sufferings of Thomas W. Smith, 1844

Being thus ingulfed in the whale's mouth and threatened with immediate destruction by the shutting of his jaws, which stood erect eight feet above water exhibiting two tremendous rows of teeth the sight of which were sufficient to dismay and terrify our hearts, there was but one alternative for us if we would save ourselves and that was to take a hold of his jaw which was one foot from my shoulder, and keep the boat from touching his teeth. This was the most important thing to be done as he was only waiting for something to touch his teeth in order to crush it in a moment; and as I was the nearest to it, it came to my lot to perform this most dangerous duty, and seeing our immediate, and imminent danger I did not hesitate, but instantly rose and stood upon the gun-wale of the boat, placing each of my hands and fingers between each row of teeth and kept the boat off, and at the same time pushed the boat ahead and she cleared the whale.

Mother love

I went forth one morning, accompanied by my ever-faithful Yamba and the usual admiring crowd of blacks ... When we were some miles from land I noticed a dark-looking object on the surface of the water a little way ahead. Feeling certain it was a dugong feeding on the well-known 'grass', I rose and hurled my harpoon at it with all the force I could muster. Next moment, to my amazement, the head of a calf whale was thrust agonisingly into the air, and not until then did I realise what manner of creature it was I had struck. This baby whale was about fifteen feet long, and it 'sounded' immediately on receiving my harpoon. As I had enough rope, or what I considered enough, I did not cut him adrift. He came up again presently, lashing the water with his tail, and creating a tremendous uproar, considering his size. He then darted off madly, dashing through the water like an arrow, and dragging our boat at such a tremendous pace as almost to swamp us in the foaming wash, the bow wave forming a kind of wall on each side.

Up to this time I had no thought of danger, but just as the baby whale halted I looked round, and saw to my horror that its colossal mother had joined her offspring, and was swimming round and round it like lightning, apparently greatly disturbed by its sufferings. Before I could even cut the line or attempt to get out of the way, the enormous creature caught sight of our little craft, and bore down upon us like a fair-sized island rushing through the sea with the speed of an express train. I shouted to Yamba, and we both threw ourselves over the side into the now raging waters, and commenced to swim away with long strokes, in order to get as far as possible from the boat before the catastrophe came which we knew was at hand. We had not got many yards before I heard a terrific crash, and, looking back, I saw the enormous tail of the great whale towering high out of the water, and my precious boat descending in fragments upon it from a height of from fifteen feet to twenty feet above the agitated waters.

Louis de Rougemont, *The Adventures of Louis de Rougemont*, 1900

Navigatio Santi Brendani Abatis
(Voyage of Saint Brendan the Abbot), 9th century

The WHALE ISLAND

When they drew nigh to the nearest island, the boat stopped ere they reached a landing-place; and the saint ordered the brethren to get out into the sea, and make the vessel fast, stem and stern, until they came to some harbour; there was no grass on the island, very little wood, and no sand on the shore. While the brethren spent the night in prayer outside the vessel, the saint remained in it, for he knew well what manner of island was this; but he wished not to tell the brethren, lest they might be too much afraid. When morning dawned, he bade the priests to celebrate Mass, and after they had done so, and he himself had said Mass in the boat, the brethren took out some uncooked meat and fish they had brought from the other island, and put a cauldron on a fire to cook them. After they had placed more fuel on the fire, and the cauldron began to boil, the island moved about like a wave; whereupon they all rushed towards the boat, and implored the protection of their father, who, taking each one by the hand, drew them all into the vessel; then relinquishing what they had removed to the island, they cast their boat loose, to sail away, when the island at once sunk into the ocean.

Afterwards they could see the fire they had kindled still burning more than two miles off, and then Brendan explained the occurrence: 'Brethren, you wonder at what has happened to this island', 'Yes, father', said they: 'we wondered, and were seized with a great fear'. 'Fear not, my children', said the saint, 'for God has last night revealed to me the mystery of all this; it was not an island you were upon, but a fish, the largest of all that swim in the ocean, which is ever trying to make its head and tail meet, but cannot succeed, because of its great length. Its name is Iasconius'.

Middle English Bestiary
[MIDDLE ENGLISH PHYSIOLOGUS] c.1300
The DECEIT OF THE WHALE

The whale is the largest fish that is in the ocean. You would say, if you should see it afloat, that it is an island, that sits upon the sea sand. When this fish, so unwieldy, is hungry he opens his jaws wide, and out of his throat comes a sweet odor, the sweetest thing that is on earth. When other fish perceive it they are glad to draw near; they come and hover in his mouth, unaware of his deceit. Then the whale shuts his jaws, sucking in all these fish. It is only the small ones he thus deceives; the big ones he cannot catch. This fish dwells at the bottom of the ocean, and lives there, always hale and well, until it come to be the time when storms stir all the sea. Then summer and winter contend, and the whale cannot stay there, because the sea bottom is so turbid, so he rises and lies still, while the weather is so bad. Sailors in the ships driven about on the sea, dreading to die and anxious to live, look around and see this fish, and, believing it is an island, are very happy as they draw near; with all their strength they cast anchor, and go upon the island. By flint and steel they start a fire burning well on this wonder, and warm themselves, and eat and drink. The whale, feeling the fire, sinks them, for he quickly dives down to the bottom of the sea and thus drowns them all.

THE FOURTEENTH SECTION

There be seen sometimes neere unto Island huge Whales like unto mountains, which overturne ships, unlesse they be terrified away with the sound of trumpets, or beguiled with round and emptie vessels, which they delight to tosses up and downe. It sometimes falleth out that Mariners thinking these Whales to be Ilands, and casting out ankers upon their backs, are often in danger of drowning. They are called in their tongue Trollwal Tuffelwalen, that is to say, the devilish Whale.

Richard Hakluyt, *The Principal Navigation Voyages, Traffiques & Discoveries of the English Nation*, 1600

ABOUT THE PHYSETER AND HIS GREAT CRUELTY

The physeter, which is classified as a whale and is 200 cubits long, has a very cruel nature and temperament, because usually he rises out of the water to wreck ships. He raises himself to above the sprit and blows out through the pipes on top of his head the water that he has taken in, so that with a huge tremendous flood of water he often causes the biggest and strongest ships to go under or at least puts the crew at risk of drowning. He has a black and thick skin all over his body, long fins like wide feet, and a forked tail, which is 15 or 20 feet wide and with which he holds the ships very tightly. Nevertheless the seamen have a very effective remedy against malice, and that is a trumpet. He cannot stand its loud and harsh sound at all. As a second remedy they also throw tremendously large barrels into the sea with which they try to stop the beast from approaching because he starts to play with these barrels. They also fire large pieces of artillery to frighten the beast with the din rather than to wound it, because iron or stone cannonballs lose their power in the water and also have little capacity to harm such a large body because of the animal's layer of fat.

Adriaen Coenen, *The Whale Book*, 1585

ABOUT A BIG FISH THAT SWALLOWED A SMALL BOAT WITH TWO MEN ON BOARD

I was told, and assured that it was true, that a big ship was once anchored off Norway. Two of the crew went out sailing in a small boat or sloop for pleasure because it was fine weather. While they were sailing, a big fish came along that swallowed the boat, men and all. But because the big fish couldn't digest the boat and was troubled by it, he was washed up and floated back and forth just off the coast. The people who lived there came and cut it open and chopped the fish in pieces. Once it had been opened, they found a small boat in the fish with two men: one was dead, the other was still alive. The one who was still alive had been near the front close to the fish's mouth. His hair had been singed off his head by the heat; the dead man had been buried deeper in the body.

Adriaen Coenen, *The Whale Book*, 1585

The mighty mass of gristle

At first the proceedings were quite of the usual character, our chief wielding his lance in most brilliant fashion, while not being fast to the animal allowed us much greater freedom in our evolutions; but that fatal habit of the mate's — of allowing his boat to take care of herself so long as he was getting in some good home thrusts — once more asserted itself. Although the whale was exceedingly vigorous, churning the sea into yeasty foam over an enormous area, there we wallowed close to him, right in the middle of the turmoil, actually courting disaster.

He had just settled down for a moment, when, glancing over the gunwale, I saw his tail, like a vast shadow, sweeping away from us towards the second mate, who was laying off the other side of him. Before I had time to think, the mighty mass of gristle leapt into the sunshine, curved back from us like a huge bow. Then with a roar it came at us, released from its tension of Heaven knows how many tons. Full on the broadside it struck us, sending every soul but me flying out of the wreckage as if fired from catapults. I did not go because my foot was jammed somehow in the well of the boat, but the wrench nearly pulled my thigh-bone out of its socket. I had hardly released my foot, when, towering above me, came the colossal head of the great creature, as he ploughed through the bundle of débris that had just been a boat. There was an appalling roar of water in my ears, and darkness that might be felt all around. Yet, in the midst of it all, one thought predominated as clearly as if I had been turning it over in my mind in the quiet of my bunk aboard — 'What if he should swallow me?' Nor to this day can I understand how I escaped the portals of his gullet, which of course gaped wide as a church door. But the agony of holding my breath soon over-powered every other feeling and thought, till just as something was going to snap inside my head I rose to the surface. I was surrounded by a welter of bloody froth, which made it impossible for me to see; but oh, the air was sweet!

Frank T. Bullen, *The Cruise of the 'Cachalot'*, 1898

LOSS OF THE
Essex

The ship *Essex*, George Pollard, Master, sailed from Nantucket, in North America, August 12, 1819, on a whaling voyage to the South Seas.

The *Essex* was for some months very successful, and procured 750 barrels of oil, in a shorter period than usual.

On the 20th November, 1820, she was on the equator, about 118° west longitude, when several whales were in sight, to the great joy of the crew, who thought they should soon complete their cargo.

The boats were soon lowered in pursuit of the whales: George Pollard, the master, and Thomas Chapple, the second mate, each succeeded in striking one, and were actively engaged in securing them, when a black man, who was in the mate's boat, exclaimed, 'Massa, where ship?' The mate immediately looked round, and saw the *Essex* lying on her beam ends, and a large whale near her: he instantly cut his line and made towards the ship; the captain also saw what had happened and did the same. As soon as they got on board, to their great astonishment they found she had been struck by a whale of the largest size, which rose close to the ship and then darted under her, and knocked off a great part of the false keel. The whale appeared again, and went about a quarter of a mile off, then suddenly returned and struck the ship with great force. The shock was most violent, the bows were stove in, and the vessel driven astern a considerable distance; she filled with water and fell over on her beam ends. The crew exerted themselves to the utmost, the masts were cut away and the ship righted, but she was a mere wreck and entirely unmanageable; the quantity of oil on board alone kept her from foundering. They did not ascertain whether the whale received any injury, but it remained in sight for some hours without again coming near them.

Owen Chase, *Shipwreck of the Whaleship* Essex, 1821

❧

We now come to give an account of the shipwreck of the *Essex* and subsequent sufferings of the crew whilst lingering in their whale boats.

Nothing occurred from our last untill the morning of the 20th November when all hands was suddenly aroused by a cry from the man at the mast head of [']Whales.['] The boats were instantly lowerd and in full persuit. The boat of the chief mate soon came up with and attacked a small whale, when with the flourish of its tail the boat was badly stoven on one side, and was filling very rapidly with water when each of us in the boat stripd off our shirts and cramd [them] into the hole which was broken. This prevented the boat from sinking and gave us an opportunity to return to the ship in our own boat.

The other two boats had alreadey got amongst the whales in an other direction and had fastend to two of them, being then about two miles to le[e]ward from the ship. In the mean time we had got our broken boat to the ship having hoisted her upon the cranes and the mate at work repairing the breach temporarily, when I being then at the helm and looking on the windward side of the ship saw a very large whale approaching us.

I calld out to the mate to inform him of it. On his seeing the whale he instantly gave me an order to put the helm hard up, and steer down towards the boats. I had scarcely time to obey the order, when I heard a loud cry from several voices at once, that the whale was coming foul of the ship. Scarcely had the sound of their voices reached my ears when it was followed by a tremendous crash. The whale had struck the ship with his head directly under the larboard fore chains at the waters edge with such force as to shock every man upon his feet.

The whale then setting under the ships bottom came up on the starboard side and directly under the starboard quarter. This last position gave the mate a fine opportunity to have killd him with a throw of his lance. His first impulse was to do so, but on a second look observing his tail directly beneath the rudder his better judgment prevaild lest a flourish of the tail should unhang the rudder and render the ship unmanagable. But could he have foreseen all that so soon followed he would probably have chosen the lesser evil and have saved the ship by killing the whale even at the expense of losing the rudder. For as we will show all wasnot yet over.

Instead of leaving the ship, the monster took a turn off about three hundred yards ahead, then turning short around came with his utmost speed and again struck the ship a tremendous blow with his head upon the larboard bow and with such force as to stave in the whole bow at the waters-edge.

One of the men who was below at the time, came running upon deck saying the ship is filling with water. The first order was to try the pumps, but of this they were spared the trouble, for on going to the hatchway it was discoverd that alreadey had the water appe[a]red above the lower deck, which on discovering we turned our attention to getting clear the boat, which was stowed overhead and bottom upwards, that being the only boat left us, with which we could expect to escape.

This was no easey task, under the present excitement. Nevertheless we succeeded in getting her out without injury, although the ship was waterlogd, and fast falling upon her side.

In the mean time the steward hadnot been idle. He had twice enterd the cabin under the most trying circumstances and at his peril, had brot out the trunks of the captain and mate and also two quadrants and two of Bowditch Practical Navigators. These, with the two compasses taken from the binnacle, was all, that we had an opportunity of getting into the boat, and get in ourselves when the ship capsized, with the mast heads in the water.

The scene at this moment — no one can ever realize to its extent, unless they have been in such a situation under similar circumstances. What an association of ideas flashed across our minds on the instant. Here lay our beautiful ship, a floating and dismal wreck, — which but a few minutes before appeard in all her glory, the pride and boast of her capt and officers, and almost idolized by her crew, with all sails neatly set and trimd to the breeze presenting to the eye the fac similie of a ship about to leave the harbour on a summers day under the admiring gaze of hundreds to witness such a scene.

Here she now lays, snatched untimely from her stateliness, into a mere shadow of what she was, and our selves deprived of the home which her goodly sides had so long afforded us.

Thomas Nickerson's account of the loss of the *Essex*, 1820

DEATH OF CAPTAIN AHAB

The harpoon was darted; the stricken whale flew forward; with igniting velocity the line ran through the grooves; — ran foul. Ahab stooped to clear it; he did clear it; but the flying turn caught him round the neck, and voicelessly as Turkish mutes bowstring their victim, he was shot out of the boat, ere the crew knew he was gone. Next instant, the heavy eye-splice in the rope's final end flew out of the stark-empty tub, knocked down an oarsman, and smiting the sea, disappeared in its depths.

Herman Melville, *Moby Dick*, 1851

IN LEVIATHAN'S *wake* THE WHALES COMPANION

Canst thou draw out leviathan with a hook?

or his tongue with a cord which thou lettest down?

Canst thou put a hook into his nose?

or bore his jaw through with a thorn?

Will he make many supplications unto thee?

Will he speak soft words unto thee?

Will he make a covenant with thee?

Wilt thou take him for a servant for ever?

Wilt thou play with him as with a bird?

Or wilt thou bind him for thy maidens?

Shall the companions make a banquet of him?

Shall they part him among the merchants?

Canst thou fill his skin with barbed irons?

or his head with fish spears?

Job: 41

Whitherward now in roaring gales?
Competing still, ye huntsman-whalers,
In leviathan's wake what boat prevails?

Herman Melville, 'John Marr and other Sailors', 1888

The Whale's *way*

My heart leaps within me
My mind roams with the waves
Over the whale's domain, it wanders far and wide
Across the face of the earth, returns again to me
Eager and unsatisfied; the solitary bird screams,
Irresistible, urges the heart to the whale's way
Over the stretch of seas

Anonymous English poem, 9th century

WICKED, set *little* eye

RUDYARD KIPLING, *Captains Courageous,* 1897

Pushing, shoving, and hauling, greeting old friends here and warning old enemies there, Commodore Tom Platt led his little fleet well to leeward of the general crowd, and immediately three or four men began to haul on their anchors with intent to lee-bow the 'We're Heres.' But a yell of laughter went up as a dory shot from her station with exceeding speed, its occupant pulling madly on the roding.

'Give her slack!' roared twenty voices. 'Let him shake it out.'

'What's the matter?' said Harvey, as the boat flashed away to the southward. 'He's anchored, isn't he?'

'Anchored, sure enough, but his graound-tackle's kinder shifty,' said Dan, laughing. 'Whale's fouled it ... Dip, Harve! Here they come!'...

Then everybody shouted and tried to haul up his anchor to get among the school, and fouled his neighbour's line and said what was in his heart, and dipped furiously with his dip-net, and shrieked cautions and advice to his companions, while the deep fizzed like freshly-opened soda water, and cod, men, and whales together flung in upon the luckless bait. Harvey was nearly knocked overboard by the handle of Dan's net. But in all the wild tumult he noticed, and never forgot, the wicked, set little eye — something like a circus-elephant's eye — of a whale that drove along almost level with the water, and, so he said, winked at him. Three boats found their rodings fouled by these reckless mid-sea hunters, and were towed half a mile ere their horses shook the line free.

Revenge of the SEA

And, after all, even now man is by no means such a master of the kingdoms of life as he is apt to imagine. The sea, that mysterious nursery of living things, is for all practical purposes beyond his control. The low-water mark is his limit. Beyond that he may do a little with seine and dredge, murder a few million herrings a year as they come in to spawn, butcher his fellow air-breather, the whale, or haul now and then an unlucky king-crab or strange sea-urchin out of the deep water, in the name of science; but the life of the sea as a whole knows him not, plays out its slow drama of change and development unheeding him, and may in the end, in mere idle sport, throw up some new terrestrial denizens, some new competitor for space to live in and food to live upon, that will sweep him and all his little contrivances out of existence, as certainly and inevitably as he has swept away auk, bison, and dodo during the last two hundred years.

H. G. Wells, 'The Extinction of Man', *Certain Personal Matters*, 1898

WHALE BONES

I built a cottage for Susan and myself, and made a gateway in the form of a Gothic arch, by setting up a whale's jaw-bones ... I am a spinner of long yarns. Seated on the gunwale of a dory, or on the sunny side of a boat-house, where the warmth is grateful to my limbs, or by my own hearth, when a friend or two are there, I overflow with talk, and yet am never tedious. With a broken voice I give utterance to much wisdom ... I give the history of the great whale that was landed on Whale Beach, and whose jaws, being now my gateway, will last for ages after my coffin shall have passed beneath them.

Nathaniel Hawthorne, *The Village Uncle*, 1837

Picture captions

Endpapers: Edouard Travies (1809–c.1865), *Adam and Eve and the Animals*, 1841, pen and ink on paper, private collection, Archives Charmet/The Bridgeman Art Library

Page 2: French print of *The Vessel Runs Low by the Boarding of a Whale*, 16th century

Page 3: *Comparative sizes of blue whale and human diver*, unattributed

Page 4: Edward Lear (1812–1888), *The Letter W*, one of 26 drawings from *A Children's Nonsense Alphabet*, c.1880, pen and Indian ink

Page 5: Left: M. Dubourg (fl. 1786–1808), *A ships boat attacking a whale*, London, published and sold by Edwd. Orme, Feby. 1st, 1813. 1 print: aquatint, hand col.; plate mark 18 x 22.8 cm
Right· James Hulett, *Nature Displayed*, (detail) 1763, engraving

Page 6: *A Whale in Trafalgar Square*, c.1930, pen and ink
C. A. Ferrieris, *Humpback whale suckling her young*, engraving

Page 9: James Hulett, *Nature Displayed*, 1763, engraving

Page 10: *Sea creatures*, 1755

Page 11: *Sea creatures*, 1755

Page 12: *Medieval sailors mistake a sleeping whale for an island, disembark in order to cook their lunch*, miniature from the Bestiare d'Amour of Richard Furnival, 10th century

Page 13: *A whale skeleton on display in Paris*, 19th century, drawn and engraved by Adam, lithograph by de Benard

Page 15: Louis Sargent, *A sperm whale Physeter macrocephalus*, in *Wild Beasts of the World*, 1909

Page 21: *Five sailors in a threemasked boat looking at a large fish with a wave breaking over its back*, 1595, Turkish miniature, Ms Harley 5500, fol. 126

Page 23: *Two whales*, 17th century

Page 24: *Whaling*, 19th century

Page 27: *Dolphin foetus and gnarled whale*, 1837-1840

Page 28: *Ilustration depicting various aquatic mammals, including the walrus, the sea lion, and the spermaceti whale*, colour lithograph, undated

Pages 30–31: Jean Marc Cote, *A whale-bus*, 1899

Page 32: *A whale from Greenland*, in The Royal Natural History, undated

Pages 34–35: *Sperm Whale Fishery*, unattributed

Page 38: *Sperm whales caught*, unattributed

Page 41: *The skeleton of a sperm whale*, 19th century

Page 43: *A school of sperm whales*, c.1820, engraving

Pages 44–45: *The muskox, Bos moschatus./Bowhead whale, Balaena mysticetus*, pen and ink coloured lithograph, plate 58 from Schreiber's *Bilder-Werke für den Anschauungs-Unterricht*, 6 vols, Wilde Tiere aller Zonen, Esslingen (J. F. Schreiber), no date (c.1850)

Page 46: *A spouting WHALE-FISH suckles its young, while a SEA-PIG watches with interest*, 1558

Pages 220–21: Japanese School, *The Jointing of a Whale*, late 19th century, colour engraving, private collection, Archives Charmet/The Bridgeman Art Library

Page 222: After George Angas (1822–1886), *Natives of Encounter Bay, making cord for fishing nets in a hut formed from the ribs of a whale, from 'South Australia Illustrated'*, published in 1847, hand coloured engraving, private collection, The Stapleton Collection/The Bridgeman Art Library

Page 224: E. A. Tilly, *Cutting up a whale – gathering spermaceti from the head*, c.1880, engraving

Page 227: *Illustration of 'There Was a Whale' From L. Frank Baum's, 'Father Goose, His Book'*, 1899

Page 229: French School, *Whaling implements*, 18th century, colour engraving, private collection, Archives Charmet/The Bridgeman Art Library

Page 230: Nicholas Mau, *Whale Song*, 1992

Page 239: *Sperm Whale at Sea*, 1890, engraving

Page 241: *Sixty whales attack a German liner 'Prinz Sigismund' in the Atlantic, but it escapes them*, published in Le Petit Journal, 17 August 1913

Page 249: A. Burnham Shute, *Illustration of the White Whale*, c.1851

Pages 254–55: 'The muskox, Bos moschatus./ Bowhead whale, Balaena mysticetus', pen and ink lithograph, coloured, plate 58 from Schreiber's *Bilder-Werke für den Anschauungs-Unterricht*, 6 vols, Wilde Tiere aller Zonen, Esslingen (J. F. Schreiber), no date (c.1850)

Page 257: Cover illustration from *Twenty Thousand Leagues Under the Sea* by Jules Verne (1828–1905), engraved by Henri Theophile Hildibrand (1824–1897) after Edouard Riou (1833–1900)

Page 258: Jonathan Langley (b.1952), *He found one single, solitary shipwrecked mariner, trailing his toes in the water*, illustration to *How the Whale got his Throat* from *Just So Stories* by Rudyard Kipling, published by Methuen Children's Books, 1989, private collection, © Chris Beetles, London, UK/The Bridgeman Art Library.

Page 261: *Right whale spouting*, hand-coloured woodcut

Index of sources

ACKNOWLEDGEMENTS

Images
AKG images: pages 21, 44–45, 138, 141, 202, 254–55
Australpress/topfoto: pages 24, 58, 78, 87, 108, 162, 217
Corbis: pages 28, 100–101, 102, 142, 143, 151, 184, 192, 195, 210, 227, 249
Getty images: pages 3, 43, 49, 52, 56, 107, 115, 117, 130–131, 136, 182–83
National Gallery of Australia: page 113
National Library of Australia: page 5
Photolibrary.com: pages 2, 6, 8, 12, 13, 15, 23, 30–31, 32, 38, 41, 46, 54–55, 59, 64, 65, 68, 71, 72, 75, 82–83, 84, 88, 112, 123, 124, 127, 132, 135, 136, 140, 147, 148–49, 152, 155, 161, 170, 171, 173, 174, 179, 180, 181, 187, 188–89, 191, 207, 212, 216, 220–21, 222, 224, 229, 238, 239, 241, 257, 258, endpapers
Science and Society Photo Library: pages 27, 32–33, 67
State Library of Tasmania: pages 204–205
State Library of Victoria: page 230
V&A Museum: page 4

Text
Every effort has been made to trace and contact the copyright holders prior to publication. If notified, the publisher undertakes to rectify any errors or omissions at the earliest opportunity. The publisher gratefully acknowledges the following sources:

Page 25: 'Fastitocalon', *The Old English Physiologus*, Albert S. Cook and James Hall Pitman, Yale University Press, 1921

Pages 26–27, 186, 223, 248: *The Whale Book: Whales and other marine animals as described by Adriaen Coenen in 1585*, edited and introduction by Florike Egmond and Peter Mason with commentaries by Kees Lankester, Reaktion Books, London 2003

Page 49: 'Whale', *Selected Poems of Anne Sexton*, 2000. Reprinted by permission of SII/Sterling Lord Literistic, Inc.

Page 53: 'Spout and Song', Kenneth Brower in *The Presence of Whales*, Frank Stewart, Alaska Northwest Books, 1995

Page 56: *The Sea-Raiders*, H. G. Wells, originally published in *The Weekly Sun Literary Supplement*, 6 December 1896

Page 60: 'Bubble Netting', *The Whale's Journey*, Stephen Martin, Allen and Unwin, 2001

Page 61: 'Voyage of The Kon-Tiki', *Kon-Tiki: Across The Pacific By Raft*, Thor Heyerdahl, Rand McNally & Company, 1950

Pages 72–73: 'Thorhall's Reward', *The Vinland Sagas: The Norse Discovery of America*, Magnus Magnusson, Penguin Classics, 1965

Page 93: 'King Sulemani and The Whale', this retelling based on an account on www.worldtrans.org

Pages 94–95: 'The Whale Man and His Canoe', *Gadi Mirrabooka*, Francis Firebrace Jones, 2001. Reproduced with permission of Greenwood Publishing Group, Inc., Westport, CT

Pages 96–97: 'Turtle, Oyster and Whale', *Aboriginal Myths, Legends and Fables*, A. W. Reed, 1978

Pages 98–99: 'Tinirau and His Pet Whale', *Maori Legends*, Alistair Campbell, Seven Seas Publishing, 1969

Pages 102–105: *The Whale Rider*, Witi Ihimaera, Reed Publishing (NZ) Ltd, 1987. Reprinted with permission of the Penguin Group (NZ)

Page 106: 'Inuit myth', *Myths, Legends and Folklores of America*, David Leeming and Jake Page, Oxford University Press, 1999

Page 111: *The Golden Bough*, Sir James George Frazer, MacMillan, 1922

Page 117: 'The Whale', *The Bad Child's Book of Beasts*, Hilaire Belloc, 1896

Pages 124–125: 'Hitchhiker's Guide to Whales', *The Hitchhiker's Guide to the Galaxy*, Douglas Adams, Pan MacMillan, 1979

Page 136: 'Whale', *Black Slang: A Dictionary of Afro-American Talk*, Clarence Major, Taylor & Francis Books Ltd, 1978

Page 138: Extract from *Ulysses* by James Joyce printed with permission of the Estate of James Joyce

Page 139: 'Spermaceti', copyright © Les Murray, 1992 used with kind permission of the author

Pages 166–169: 'The Wellfleet Whale', from *Passing Through: The later poems new and selected*, Stanley Kunitz, 1985. Used with permission of W. W. Norton & Company Inc.

Page 208: 'Slaughter of the Beast', *Coast of Coral and Pearl*, Peter Lancaster Brown, 1972. First published in Britain by Robert Hale Ltd

Page 217: 'Gulathing Law', *Bad to the Bone: The Unnatural History of Monstrous Medieval Whales*, Vicki Ellen Szabo, 2005

Page 231: 'Where Went That Spirit?', *Whaling North and South*, F. V. Morley, Century, 1926

Pages 234–235: 'No Humane Way To Kill A Whale', weblog, copyright © Tim Winton. The author of 20 books, Tim Winton is the patron of the Australian Marine Conservation Society

Page 260: 'Revenge of The Sea', from 'The Extinction of Man', in *Certain Personal Matters*, H. G. Wells, Lawrence & Bullen, 1898

First published in 2008 by Pier 9, an imprint of Murdoch Books Pty Ltd

Murdoch Books Australia
Pier 8/9
23 Hickson Road
Millers Point NSW 2000
Phone: +61 (0) 2 8820 2000
Fax: + 61 (0) 2 8220 2558
www.murdochbooks.com.au

Murdoch Books UK Limited
Erico House, 6th Floor
93–99 Upper Richmond Road
Putney, London SW15 2TG
Phone: +44 (0) 20 8785 5995
Fax: +44 (0) 20 8785 5985
www.murdochbooks.co.uk

Chief Executive: Juliet Rogers
Publishing Director: Kay Scarlett

Commissioning Editor: Diana Hill
Editor and additional text: Ariana Klepac
Concept and design: Emilia Toia
Text researchers: Ariana Klepac, Amanda Jane Smith
Picture researcher: Amanda McKittrick
Rights and permissions: Jacqui Smith
Production: Monique Layt

National Library of Australia Cataloguing-in-Publication Data
Author: Klepac, Ariana.
Title: The whales companion/Ariana Klepac.
ISBN: 9781741960402 (hbk.)
Notes: Includes index.
Subjects: Whales. Whales in art. Whales in literature. Whales — Effect of human beings on.
Dewey Number: 599.5

Printed by 1010 Printing International Limited. PRINTED IN CHINA. First printed in 2008.